GENDER AT WORK

T0352769

Ann Game & Rosemary Pringle

Photography by Helen Grace

GENDER AT WORK

Routledge
Taylor & Francis Group

LONDON AND NEW YORK

First published 1983 by Allen & Unwin

Published 2020 by Routledge
2 Park Square, Milton Park, Abingdon, Oxon OX14 4RN
605 Third Avenue, New York, NY 10017

Routledge is an imprint of the Taylor & Francis Group, an informa business

National Library of Australia
Cataloguing-in-Publication entry:

Game, Ann.
Gender at Work.
Bibliography.
Includes Index.
IBSN 0 86861 253 7.
ISBN 0 86861 261 8 (pbk.).
1. Women—Employment—Australia.
2. Sex discrimination in employment—Australia.
I. Pringle, Rosemary. II. Grace, Helen.
III. Title
331.4′133′0994

Library of Congress Catalog Card Number: 82-83578

Phototypeset in Linotron 202 by
Graphicraft Typesetters Hong Kong

ISBN-13: 9780868612614 (pbk)

Contents

Foreword

THIS book, *Gender at Work*, makes a definitive contribution to feminist theory concerning women in the labour force in the period since World War II. I had the pleasure of reading the work in progress and now have the honour of writing a foreword. My own research goes back to the turn of the century and the pattern has changed very little. The general standard of living has gone up but the change in women's status has been slight.

Moral, social and legal codes have been based upon myths and traditions which had scant relevance to reality but have served to reinforce power. In the last 20 years women have been searching for evidence, exploding myths and rewriting history which had mostly ignored the role of women. *Gender at Work* will be welcomed for its enormous significance to activists and theoreticians alike. It was a courageous undertaking to examine current practices in the workforce especially the effects of modern technology. A great need has existed for such a reference book.

Four main precepts have determined women's condition in the workforce. First, women's skills have been denied. Secondly, women have been regarded as invaders of the workforce. Thirdly, there is the paternalism of working men, employers and the courts. Finally, the segregation of the sexes at work has made it easier to deny women equitable pay.

Taking the first, I wince at the word 'deskilling', implying as it does that the only skilled work is that which has been labelled as such. What is skill? In workforce practices skill is that which has been recognised as such by masters and men. Male gender decided. This decision had been reinforced by formal apprenticeship available to males only, thus preserving not only the status of the occupation but its male line of succession. Work performed by a female automatically failed to qualify as a trade. Men who did ironing were called pressers and considered highly skilled. Women who ironed for a living were unskilled. The sexes never worked together in this occupation. Where the sexes did work together, for example in tailoring, a male coathand was considered far superior to a female coathand. When a white man developed manual dexterity, it became a skilled trade, when a woman or a black developed manual dexterity, it was a natural characteristic and clas-sified as unskilled. The Negro tobacco stemmers in Virginia and the women stemmers working for W.D. & H.O. Wills in Britain, would have been surprised that white male tobacco stemmers in Sydney in the early 1900s considered themselves tradesmen and formed a craft union. My sister sewing pintucks at speed used as much precision and skill as a fitter tempering a piece of steel. Every occupation requires skill. Even in shovelling dirt or digging trenches, there is an enormous difference between the expert and the novice. Women in office work were denied their skill. We paid for training at business college where a good standard of spelling and grammar was required to learn typing and shorthand. When we worked in an office, every male was superior to us even if they had received no training.

Trades that have been so recognised are now threatened with deskilling by technological change, but the degree of skill which remains or the degree of new skill required to operate with the changes, are moot points which will be decided by a number of factors—the case put up by the union advocates, the supply of labour available and traditional values.

Examples in the trades illustrate the way in which women were swindled in the past in recognition of their skill. Tailoring was the only trade wherein women held the status of journeywomen. They were never paid the rate of journeymen, even when doing the same work. After two years women could become trouserhand or vesthand, and after three years, coathand. That was as far as they could go. Males served a five year apprenticeship which added cutting and pressing to the tailoring. Men preserved the skills of cutter, presser and tailor as exclusive male dominions. No matter how good they proved to be, and they were quicker at sewing than the men, it was absolutely untenable that women should receive the same wages as men. The price of labour was determined by sex, not by the value of the work, nor the competence of the worker.

In Sydney in 1890, by agreement between the journeymen tailors and the employers, a tailor was permitted to have two journeywomen working under his supervision and adding to his status. He received an additional bonus in his pay on their output. By 1904 the ratio crept up to one tailor to six tailoresses who were no longer apprenticed. Men had resisted what they considered the invasion of women but the employers wanted them because they were cheaper. There was a constant battle to fix a ratio of females to males but in the clothing trade the men did not succeed. They kept women down in the trade but not out of the industry.

In the boot trade women were also denied their skill. At the Royal Commission on Strikes held in Sydney in 1890, shoemaker George Garton gave evidence. He told the Commission that most footwear had been imported in the early days of the colony, but whatever footwear had been made here had often been done by women in the home. The husband/father, as had been the custom in England, bought the material and equipment, chased after orders, measured the customer, made the delivery and collected the money, whilst the wife and daughters made the boots. The witness, himself a good tradesman, said the women were more skilled than most men in the trade. When boot factories mushroomed in Sydney and Melbourne, women received no recognition for their skill. They were prevented from performing certain parts of the trade and restricted to specific operations delegated to them by the male workers and agreed to by factory owners. Women were used as complementary assistants to 'skilled' male operatives.

The second precept, that working women were regarded as interlopers and men did not want them in the workforce, is demonstrated by a case before the NSW Industrial Arbitration Court in 1907 concerning the boot trade. Three separate craft unions (males) made a combined claim to the Arbitration Court: they were the Boot Operators and Rough Stuff Cutters Union, the NSW Clickers Union and the Boot Trades Union of NSW. The advocate was the rising star, George Stephenson Beeby, Women were working in the same factories as the men so that men union members had every opportunity to entrol the women if they wanted to. Lest any doubts linger that women were not wanted, I quote Beeby himself from the court transcripts:

> The cases taken together are of considerable importance as they affect one of the best developed, largest and best organised industries in the State. The number of men and boys in the industry at the end of 1906 was 2600 and of women 1550. There has been expansion and the figures are now 3000 and 1600 respectively. As to the female operators, they are not in any way affected by the claims to the court. They are not organised to any extent, and at present we do not propose to ask the court to interfere in any way as to their conditions. Probably 95 per cent of the male labour is organised...

Although women were more than half the workforce, they were being left aside. No claim was made for them, they would not share in any wage increase. No automatic wage flow-on operated in those days.

A common means of rejection was the denial of apprenticeships to women. Although the number of apprentices in Sydney during 1896 for females and males had been about equal (608 and 640 respectively), by 1901 female apprenticeship had died out. The earlier apprenticeships for women had been bunched mostly in clothing and footwear but when the factories increased in number, they did not bother to apprentice females at all. In the meantime, females were specifically forbidden by many awards to take up apprenticeships in other industries where they were working, such as confectionery, leather trade and food production.

Thirdly, we come to paternalism which was best displayed in the labour movement by women's friends and colleagues, well-meaning, sentimental socialists like W.G. Spence, Harry Holland and William Lane. They all spoke and wrote of the plight of 'our sisters' in the working class who were nevertheless warned not 'to go too far' by proclaiming themselves feminists. Lane took it upon himself to write a women's column under the pseudonym of Lucinda Sharpe because women could not be trusted to speak for themselves. Men believed it their right to represent women and speak on their behalf. Women were never listened to but told what to do.

Classical examples of paternalism came from the pre-World War I arbitration judges, Higgins and Heydon. Higgins made the oft quoted statement that tailoresses were invaders of the workforce and asked what should be done with these gentle ladies. He made a great departure from convention when he granted equal pay for fruit pickers in 1912 but he regarded it as an exception—isolated, seasonal and rural. Heydon would not curtail women's right to work, nor even fix a ratio of female to male as some unions wanted him to do. It is difficult to be sure whether Heydon's attitude was based solely on paternalism or whether it was a deliberate ploy in support of the employers. His degree of awareness becomes irrelevant—the result was a paternalism which served the interests of the employers. Heydon clung to the notion that equal pay for the sexes was out of the question because men were breadwinners seeking protection from the arbitration court. These judges agonised over the dilemmas but their paternalism prevented them from making an objective decision. As I have said elsewhere, 'their support of the conventional myths was difficult to reconcile with equity and justice'.

Employers were paternalistic towards female employees, considering they had a right and a duty to cross-examine them about their family life and circumstances. Samuel Hordern, of Anthony Hordern and Sons Ltd, told the *Sydney Morning Herald* that he was deeply offended that his 'girls' should go on strike (the 1901 tailoresses' strike in Sydney) after he had been so good to them. He was self-righteous and liked to be considered a philanthropist. He willingly attended the Arbitration Court during the hearing of the first comprehensive claim by the Shop Assistants' Union in 1906–07, confident of the good impression he would make. He boasted that he himself interviewed and engaged all employees. He opposed the court fixing a minimum rate of pay as the union had requested, and explained why in a little anecdote. A young woman had come to him desperately seeking work. She said she might as well tell the truth, that she was married, but she was a good worker and had been earning twenty shillings a week before her marriage. Hordern asked where was her husband, because, he told the court, 'I like to see a woman looking after the house'. Her husband had sought work from Hordern the previous day without success. Hordern told them to come back and see him together. The man had been working at a tweed mill in England, a recent immigrant. Hordern offered him a job on the tweed counter at twentyfive shillings a week. He offered her a job at fifteen shillings. They would be earning forty shillings between them. A labourer's wage at the time was fortytwo shillings a week. The paternalistic employer got the labour of two people for the price of one and considered himself to be generous and concerned. If a minimum rate of pay was fixed, Hordern continued, he would not have been able to help this deserving couple. 'I would not like an award of the court to shut out anyone from getting a living—if you saw the people you would feel sorry for them.'

The fourth and last precept, that of segregation leading to low pay and severe exploitation, never roused the interest of the male trade unionists who were concerned mainly to keep women away from men's jobs. As equal pay for the sexes seeped through the arbitration system at long last in the 1970s, it became clear that the sexes needed to be doing the same work with the same classification, such as school teacher, to begin to achieve equality. The equal pay decisions were soon followed by changes in technology as is made clear in *Gender at Work*. In spite of their promises to the contrary, the computer industry put females only onto key punch work, thus reinforcing segregation with all its drawbacks and dangers to women's status. In trying to enter the male dominated industries, supposedly now open to women, changes in technology stymied us. Just as women were about to seek entry into stevedoring on the waterfront, containerisation was introduced and the wharfies were getting golden handshakes to leave the industry. The stevedoring industry authority told me that women had left their run too late. My colleague, Helen Prendergast of the Department of Labour in Tasmania, had devised a plan to introduce female labour in Tasmanian ports because of the acute shortage of work for women. The old old excuse of lack of lavatory accommodation had been put up as a barrier but Helen had a solution ready to provide portable toilets on the wharves. These became known in the women's movement as Prenda's portable potties. Technology put an end to the scheme. Desegregation is proving to be a formidable barrier, exacerbated by widespread unemployment.

I have been enormously stimulated by this book addressing itself to the present generation of working women. A long history of sexism precedes the position of women today. The past cannot be changed but looking backwards helps in assessing how much or how little we, as women, have advanced.

Edna Ryan

Acknowledgements

THIS book comes out of our participation in the Women's Employment Rights Campaign (WERC) which was formed in 1977 in the context of rising female unemployment rates and media campaigns blaming women for youth unemployment. In 1979 WERC produced a booklet *Women and Unemployment*. The industry studies on which this book is based began in 1978. The WERC group was central in the formulation of the questions which informed these studies, and WERC members other than the authors participated in these studies at various times.

Marion Jacka worked for two years on whitegoods. She was responsible for coordination of the project and a major part of the writing involved. Two reports came out of that project and are the basis of chapter 1: M. Jacka, and A. Game, (1980): 'The Whitegoods Industry: The Labour Process and the Sexual Division of Labour', Behavioural Sciences, Macquarie University, and M. Jacka, and R. Pringle, (1981): 'Survey of Workers in the Whitegoods Industry', Behavioural Sciences, Macquarie University.

Clare Gallagher undertook studies of the retail industry and nursing in the context of a report she prepared on part-time work for the Women's Coordination Unit, NSW Premier's Department, in 1981. Her work represents a substantial input to chapters 3 and 5.

In the last four years we have talked with a vast number of people who work in factories, banks, shops, computer centres and hospitals. Our main acknowledgement is to all those women and men who talked to us about their work lives and often their personal lives. In a very real sense this book is based on their experiences, and the practical knowledge that only they have. Without their participation it would not have been possible.

The banking project was initially funded by Kuring-gai College of Advanced Education. Macquarie University funded the whitegoods project and the photographs for the book. We should like to thank our friends and colleagues at these, our two workplaces, for their encouragement and support.

The AMWSU worked closely with us on the whitegoods study. They provided funds for the preparation and processing of the questionnaire for the 'Survey of Workers in the Whitegoods Industry'. They arranged meetings with organisers, shop stewards and workers in the industry, and allowed us to sit in on shop stewards' meetings. The ABEU and the CBOA provided valuable assistance and continual encouragement in our banking research. We should also like to thank the following: the ASE, ETU, FCU, SDA, Nurses' Association and Nurses' Reform Campaign.

Numerous companies and institutions organised interviews, tours of workplaces, and gave permission for photographs to be taken. We should like to thank the following: Email, Hoover, Kelvinator, Kirbys, Malleys, Philips, Simpson Pope; ANZ, Bank of NSW, Archives of the Bank of NSW, CBA, CBC, Archives of the CBC, Commonwealth Bank, National; Waltons, Woolworths; Royal Prince Alfred, Concord Repat., Prince Henry, Westmead.

Like many of the women in this book we too had a male patron. Our special thanks go to Bob Connell for convincing us that a string of working papers could develop into a book. He supported our applications for funds after we had been twice knocked back by that ultimate patriarchal body, the Australian Research Grants Committee. When we despaired of finding time or resources to continue he kept us going. Bob read, commented on, and helped us edit numerous drafts. His support has been invaluable.

Without Margaret Gibbs and Lesley Bulmer the banking and retail research wouldn't have got off the ground so quickly, and without Les Freedman we would never have understood the likes of proofing machines. Joan Greenbaum, David Varas and Jan Thompson helped us when we were lost in computer-land. Sister Webb, the nursing staff and patients of D5 were particularly patient with sociologists and photographer invading their ward. While many people have helped throughout our research and writing, the following should be mentioned: Gill Bottomley, Carol O'Donnell, Helen Grace, Gay Hawkins, Margy Jolly, Sue Kippax, Sharyn McGee, Steve McDonald, Jeannie Martin, Edna Ryan, Sue Wills. Drafts were typed by Pat Bonourvrie, Beverley Millard, Barbara Van Es, and the final copy by Heather Williams.

Finally, we should like to thank each other, without whom this book would not have been written.

Introduction

GENDER is fundamental to the way work is organised; and work is central in the social construction of gender. This is the deceptively straightforward theme of this book. Yet gender and work are rarely put together. When sociologists, political economists, or Marxists, study the labour process they invariably ignore gender. The best they can do is make a token mention of the ways in which gender is manipulated by management to create disunity in the working class. On the other hand most studies of gender, ranging from sex role theory to psychoanalysis, are not informed by political economy or anything more than a limited understanding of the labour process. Our view is that studies of gender and studies of the labour process are incomplete unless they take each other seriously.

This has a direct bearing on current debates about the relation between capitalism and patriarchy (Barrett, 1980; Sargeant, 1981). Many of the difficulties in this debate have arisen because of the tendency to conceptualise capitalism and patriarchy as two separate systems. For example, feminists who wish to stress the intractability of male domination by pointing out that it long predates capitalism, also make the sexual division of labour external to capitalism proper. Not only is the sexual division of labour treated in an ahistorical way but capitalism is defined very narrowly. In the more sophisticated accounts it is argued that the sexual division of labour has acquired an organic or institutional existence within capitalism but, even so, it is seen as something taken over by capitalism and used to its benefit. We want to argue that the sexual division of labour is not 'functional' to capitalism but, rather, is a defining feature of it, as central as wage labour or surplus value. It is probably important to stress the reverse also: the sexual division of labour as we experience it under capitalism takes highly specific forms. Much social analysis, particularly anthropological, has made assumptions about the sexual division of labour that do not apply to non-capitalist societies.

The sexual division of labour refers to the allocation of work on the basis of sex, within both the home and the workplace, as well as that division between home and workplace which has been characteristic of capitalism. This division of labour operates through a series of dichotomies which, on the one hand, refer to male and female spheres and, on the other, correspond to social divisions that are characteristic of capitalism: public/private, work/non-work, production/consumption. The sexual division of labour then, as we understand it, is not just something operating at home and work, but is much broader and a basic dynamic in capitalist societies. It is as important as class for analysing capitalism. Consequently an adequate understanding of the social relations of *work* cannot be gained by analysing the basic class relations involved and then superimposing the category of sex. It is essential to take account of the ways in which gender relations and class relations shape each other. This is as much the case in relation to work as in other spheres of social existence.

Gender and power

The aim of our project has been to develop an understanding of the relationship between gender, the labour process, and technological change.

Gender refers to the social meaning of being 'a man' or 'a woman'. It includes not only the construction of masculinity and femininity as psychological characteristics which we all share in different proportions, but more fundamental questions of identity and sexuality. By gender relations we mean the social relations between men and women. The *social* needs to be stressed from the outset because one of the most significant aspects of the discussion of gender relations is that it is imbued with a naturalistic ideology. Gender is experienced as something natural, inevitable and unchangeable. With no other social relations are references to the 'natural' biological world so constant and persistent. We also need to emphasise that we are talking about *relations*: if masculinity and femininity are *socially* constructed, they are also constructed in *relation* to each other. For example, when we talk about the sexual division of labour it is often assumed that we are just interested in women's work. What we are in fact concerned with is the historical relationship between 'men's' jobs and 'women's' jobs. Despite the fact that jobs are always allocated as male or female with either direct reference to biology or on the basis of supposed biological differences in characteristics and abilities, there is nothing static or fixed about the sexual division of labour. The content of men's work and women's work is subject to change. Changes in definitions of men's work and women's work always take place in relation to each other. There is nothing inherent in jobs that makes them either appropriately female or male. If anything remains fixed, it is the *distinction* between men's work and women's work. For example, if as a consequence of technological change, men's work becomes similar to women's work in a particular workplace, women will be allocated different jobs, and the nature of 'women's' work and 'men's' work redefined in order to maintain a distinction between them. The sexual division of labour is remarkably flexible given that it is supposed to be based on biology. Why then, if it *is* so flexible, does it continue to exist at all? The answer to this lies in the nature of the relations involved. Gender is not just about difference but about power: the domination of men and the subordination of women. This power relation is maintained by the creation of distinctions between male and female spheres—and it is the reproduction of these distinctions which accounts for the persistence of the so-called 'naturalness' of it all. It is because of this power relation that women are assumed to be much closer to nature than men. Whereas men are considered to have some agency in creating their social world, women are limited by biology—they bear children.

In this book we try to make sense of the social processes which generate changes in the sexual division of labour, and the ways in which it is reproduced. Gender identity is crucial here. Masculinity and femininity are not just psychological states or attributes of sex roles that could be easily shaken off with, say, a change or 'reversal' in roles. They run much deeper than this. Our fundamental identity is as sexed beings, men or women. And in claiming that identities are constructed through social practices such as work, we are also suggesting that sexuality is a fundamental aspect of this. For example, men's sense of self is affronted if they do 'women's' work. They feel they have not only been reduced in status but almost physically degraded. (The Freudians would call this castration anxiety.) Men who do 'women's' work may be seen as weak, effeminate or even homosexual. Men's work has to be experienced as empowering. Thus men work on new *powerful* machines; technology and masculinity are very closely connected. (A mere typewriter is a different matter.) If women move into male areas of work they are made to feel awkward in a number of ways. They may be called castrating bitches, or excluded from a pub scene. Sometimes they are accused of 'sleeping their way to the top' or denied their sexuality altogether as asexual 'career women'. Frequently they are subjected to sexual harassment, which is a means of keeping them in their place and ensuring that they stay there.

Changes in the organisation of work frequently provoke anxiety in men about the loss of power or the gaining of power by women to which they are not entitled. Power and sexuality are integral to work relations. As with all power relations, gender is constantly renegotiated and recreated. This process is particularly visible at points when work is being reorganised and new technologies introduced. By focussing on these it also becomes clear that masculinity and femininity are not fixed essences. There are different masculinities and femininities. Gender identities, like the power relations they embody, take a range of different forms.

Technology and power

In stressing the broader social relations of production we confront not only biological determinism but *technological* determinism as well. Technology does not fall readymade from the sky as an external 'cause'. It is a result of social processes. Yet the forms technology takes, and the pace with which they develop, are often assumed to be historically inevitable. Changes in the nature of work are thought to spring from some sort of technological imperative. This is analogous to the way in which gender is assumed to follow 'inevitably' from nature or biology.

Recent studies of the labour process have shown how new technologies are introduced to enhance management control over the work situation. Technology does not have an inherent dynamic of its own but is designed in the interests of particular social groups, and against the interests of others. These studies have focussed on the class dimension of the social relations of technology, the struggle for control of the labour process between capital and labour. We take this further by considering the gender context of the implementation of technology. This makes the pattern of relations and the struggle over technology and control of the labour process a more complex matter. Not only are there conflicts between management and the workforce over machines, but there are also conflicts between men and women over machines; over who, for example, is to operate them. These two sets of relations mediate, overlap, and sometimes contradict each other. It is not simply that the latter conflict distracts attention from the former, as a functionalist analysis would have it.

Considering the gender context of technology raises questions about some of the central concepts in labour process analyses. In particular, we must reconsider very carefully the idea that work has been systematically deskilled under late capitalism. Whose work? Where does that leave those whose work has never been defined as skilled? Are jobs inherently skilled or are they only acknowledged as such as a result of struggle? What about new skills, including those associated with coping with pressure and monotony? Why have women never been in a position to assert that *they too* have skills? While deskilling is an important and useful concept it needs to be applied with somewhat more caution than it frequently is; it cannot be used as an all-embracing term that encapsulates processes related to technological change. While it clearly applies to old craft skills in some areas of manufacturing there are doubts about how far it is applicable to other areas of work in, for example, the tertiary sector. An analysis which focuses on deskilling is also likely to represent the interests of the most privileged sections of the workforce to the exclusion of others. Skilled tradesmen are frequently seen to be representative of the whole workforce but most men and women work in jobs that are already deskilled, defined as unskilled or, perhaps more correctly, jobs that are not recognised as skilled.

If the deskilling hypothesis does not come to grips with the complexities of class, it is also gender blind. The definition of skill is gender biased. The process by which some jobs are defined as skilled and others as unskilled is complex, but by and large women's 'skills' are not recognised as such in the definitions of their jobs. Skilled work is men's work. To a considerable extent this is the result of trade union struggles to maintain the definition of jobs as skilled in order to preserve male wage rates. As Edna Ryan in the Foreword to this book points out, these struggles have usually taken the form of attempting to maintain the definition of jobs as male; 'male' and 'skill' have been synonymous. There is a long history to this. Trade unions argue that *re*skilling rather than *de*skilling is occurring as a result of technological change, as a basis for wage increase claims. They do not find it at all helpful for academics to insist that deskilling has taken place, without taking any account of the particular difficulties faced in new jobs. While this still largely applies to a male workforce, for example, metal workers, there are some interesting new developments where unions cover industries such as retailing which have become predominantly female. In such cases trade unions are forced into defining the skills in women's jobs, having given up on the fight to maintain the area as male.

Another example of the relation between gender and skill—or at least of the way it is experienced—is the common assumption, held by unions, that the movement of women into a male area will not only lower wages but lead to deskilling. As we will show, the reverse is frequently the case—work is 'deskilled' and then women move in. But it cannot be assumed that this will necessarily happen. As our industry studies show, the relation between feminisation and deskilling is much more complex than this. In each of our studies we consider the applicability of deskilling, specify the nature of the skills involved, and analyse the relation between 'deskilling' processes and gender relations. We take the view that general theories about technological change cannot be developed in the absence of concrete, specific studies.

The case studies

We have chosen six case studies to illustrate different aspects of the relationship between gender, the labour process and technological change. Since this has to be understood historically we have taken the entire postwar period and at times looked back further. With the exception of the whitegoods industry, the bulk of our research was conducted in Sydney. To look at whitegoods we went to Adelaide, Melbourne and Orange where some of the major companies and plants are located. For the other industries we think it reasonable to assume that our research in Sydney has a wider application.

The whitegoods industry illustrates the kind of division of labour that was established in a typical manufacturing industry with the setting up of mass production plants. A division between trades areas (entirely male) and semiskilled and unskilled process and assembly line work (where women and various migrant groups were heavily represented) was consolidated. Within the latter, there was a further sex-typing of jobs. This chapter concentrates on the rationalisations for these: heavy/light, dirty/clean, technical/nontechnical, mobile/immobile, and so on. We look at the ways in which these dichotomies are used to preserve a division of labour, the basis of which is threatened by technological changes. Whitegoods shows up clearly a process of continual redefinition of the sexual division of labour which intersects with changes in technology and the reorganisation of work.

Banking is a case of 'where have all the male middle-class careers gone'? Since World War II women have moved from being a tiny proportion of bank staff to almost half. At the same time there have been continuous changes in technology, from the ledger machine to computerisation and automatic telling. This has meant changes in the way bank work is organised, and in the career structure and employment opportunities. Here we consider the relationship between the 'proletarianisation' of white collar work, the end of opportunities for upward mobility, and the 'feminisation' of the labour force. By this we mean the increasing proportion of women employed in the industry.

Retailing too has seen a big influx of women since the late 1950s. Although it has at times been portrayed as a respectable occupation, the majority of retailing workers have never been middle class. They have struggled to preserve a view of themselves as a cut above manual labour but this has been harder to maintain as the service component went out of selling and it came to look more like factory work. We focus here on the substantial feminisation from the late 1950s, which is closely connected with the suburbanisation of the industry and with the new types of work in supermarkets. The most striking development over the last few years had been the growth of part-time (mostly casual) work at the expense of full-time jobs. This development has been made possible by the large scale presence of women.

Computing is an example of a new industry where jobs are supposedly nonsex-typed yet gender divisions are as central in the organisation of work here as elsewhere. This suggests that the sexual division of labour is not some remnant from the past that is gradually being eliminated; it is a structural feature of modern capitalism.

Nursing is a traditional women's occupation. We situate changes in nursing work in relation to the broader division of labour in the health industry. In contrast to banking there is a significant movement of men into the area, though not yet a masculinisation of equivalent proportions. We consider the significance of the professionalisation of nursing, that is, the various attempts to raise its status. One aspect of this has been the replacement of 'female' power structures (the dragon Matron) with more 'masculine' notions of bureaucratic control.

Housework, or the 'non-work' side of the work/non-work dichotomy, is of course women's work par excellence. New technology in the home does not reduce the workload for women or break down the sexual division of labour. We consider the range of new jobs that have been created in the domestic sphere by the growth of consumption. In this chapter we also challenge the masculine mode of dividing all human activity into 'work', which is valued, and 'non-work' which is not, and raise broader issues about contradictions in the construction of femininity at home and work.

Control of the labour process

Changes in the labour process and the sexual division of labour need to be understood in the context of control and its various forms.

The management 'problem' of getting workers to work involves not only maximising their output, but also obscuring the means by which this is achieved, the social relations of work. Analyses of the labour process have emphasised this, but have only identified the capital dynamic involved, and not the gender dynamic. Taking one of these author's periodisations of forms of control as a useful starting point we can read between the lines to show the centrality of gender to control of the labour process. Edwards (1979) distinguishes between three forms of control. First, there is simple control which is direct and personal and where power is invested in individuals, for example, the 'entrepreneur'. Secondly, there is technical control, where the control mechanism is designed into the machine and technology paces and directs work. And thirdly, there is bureaucratic control, where control is embedded in the social organisation of the enterprise through the use of rules, procedures, job descriptions and evaluations. Each of these forms of control is patriarchal, although Edwards, in his gender blindness, does not recognise this.

Simple control is control by the 'father', often in a symbolic sense but frequently quite literally, in small enterprises and family companies. The banks and retail stores until comparatively recently exercised, and in some cases continue to exercise, control over their workforce with the use of family imagery. The bank was meant to be 'one big happy family'. Workers were assured that 'the bank will look after them'. This interest in employees extended to personal life for the branch manager was meant to keep a check on the conduct of his staff outside work. Earlier this century bank officers were 'forbidden to live in hotels . . . or associate with persons of questionable character' and they were 'prohibited from taking a public or active part in any question which may incite strong feelings in a community, especially in political questions. . .'. (Rules and Instructions to be observed by Officers of the Commercial Banking Company of Sydney Limited, 1910.) They also had to ask permission to marry. In nursing too a simple form of control which is explicitly patriarchal has predominated throughout most of the twentieth century. The doctor and matron have been set up as the father and mother of a household.

What does this say about the public/private split? Control at work, particularly in the case of simple forms of control, also incorporated control over the private, 'non-work' sphere of life. The rigid separation of the spheres which we experience under late capitalism has grown up alongside the development of more bureaucratic modes. Sennett suggests we have moved towards subtler forms of control through indifference and impersonality rather than through direct intervention (1980: 84–121). The separation of the spheres may be seen as part of this process. Certainly the relation between public and private is historically determined. There is nothing fixed or inevitable about it.

Technical control is patriarchal in a less direct though no less powerful sense than simple control. Machines, particularly new ones, are represented as masculine. It is perhaps ironical that men are frequently put on to new machines because 'women don't understand them', given the extent to which 'skills' are actually incorporated into the machines. Men too are being controlled by capital's masculine machines—but the masculinity of them goes some way to disguising this. Smaller machines, such as proofing machines, word processors and terminals, are operated by women. But behind these looms the computer, the real source of power.

Bureaucratic control is the form frequently preferred by women. They can say, 'we don't need a male patron; we can make it on merit'. Women in the private banks sometimes envy women in the Commonwealth Bank with its Public Service Appeal System. This form of control operates through denial that there is any discrimination. It is asserted that gender is irrelevant, that women can make it on the same terms as men, that all will be rationally and fairly evaluated, according to the same criteria. This ignores the specific problems faced by women workers and the ways in which the whole world of work is structured around male norms. It operates precisely by saying 'we are not interested in anything about you except whether you can do the job', that is, through indifference. 'Rational' control is subtler, but no less patriarchal, than the other forms. It is embodied in the ideology that 'women can make it in a man's world' and that they can prove themselves at men's work as long as they retain their femininity. Women in banks with new 'equal opportunities' images have learnt that the power structure is still very much a male power structure, however rational and anonymous it may seem. We can call this 'Patriarchy without the Father' to signify that it comes from an apparently neutral system. In some ways it is harder to fight, for it operates on denial of the authority relations, it is impersonal and no one can be held directly responsible. Men can be let off the hook or claim that they too are victims. Therein lies its strength and flexibility.

What does it mean to say that control in the workplace is patriarchal? Patriarchy is a structure that gives some men power over other men, and *all* men power over women. Men at the bottom of the male hierarchy still fight to retain this power. Those at the top often assert it even when it seems to be in contradiction to their economic interests. Just as they will often forego surplus value if necessary to increase their control over the labour process, they will forego it also to maintain the sexual division of labour. It is in this sense that we can say that the inner logic of capital is patriarchal. Capitalist rationality is based on male dominance.

The sexual division of labour and gender identification operate as a means of social control both in conscious and not so conscious ways. Management deliberately employ women so that they will be able to handle job loss by 'natural wastage', or to get maximum tedious work done by the cheapest labour, or disguise the effects of technology on the nature of work. But there is a much more subtle dimension to all of this. It relates to what we have said previously about the construction of gender identity, which is, in many ways an unconscious process. If management derive benefits from a patriarchal structure so also do male workers. This is not to suggest that male workers have the same interests as management and there are plenty of cases of conflict between them over what form the sexual division of labour should take. It would be a mistake to view the sexual division of labour as a management plot, or as a structure imposed on the workforce from on high. Male workers accept it and women workers find difficulty in initiating more than limited resistance. Both men and women are actively involved in reproducing it in the way they go about their daily lives, both at work, and outside the workplace.

The contradictory nature of the construction of masculinity is central here. Masculinity is very much connected with the world of work and yet for working class men their experience of work is an alienating one. On the one hand men work via their identity as breadwinners and on the other hand they are subjected to relations in work that potentially threaten this identity. One of the ways in which men's sense of power and control is maintained is in relation to women's position in the home, that is, through the power relation involved in the sexual division of labour in the family. The other way is through the sexual division of labour in the workplace. Men's jobs give them an illusion of control in relation to women's jobs. It should be pointed out that even when management consciously use a strategy of a sexual division of labour as a means of controlling the labour process, it is not a matter of *imposing* it. They do not have to. It is experienced as *natural*, both in the workplace, and in the so-called private sphere of life.

In our industry studies we originally set out to investigate the ways in which a sexual division of labour obscures changes in the labour process designed to increase management control, such as the introduction of machines which remove decision-making power from the workforce. It has become clear in the course of our research that this question does not go far enough and that it remains within the terms of the old debate about whether or not the sexual division of labour is functional to capitalism. Finally we realised that gender is *built in* at the level of the production/consumption division and in the way in which the labour process is organised, and that to understand this we would have to look at the economic in relation to the sexual and the symbolic. We do not have to prove that capitalism uses the sexual division of labour to increase profits and divide the working class. It is not 'functional' to capitalism in this one-to-one way but rather is a central part *of* it. This distinction became profoundly important to us, for it meant rejecting the possibility of a 'non-patriarchal' capitalism and insisting that we cannot think capitalism without gender.

The complexities of the power relations involved emerged when we tried to make sense of men's and women's experiences of gender relations, and the particular division of labour in each workplace. At times there appeared to be no logic at all to the way work was organised and jobs divided. This was partly because we tended to look just for the capital logic in a division of labour. There were anomalies, or apparent ones, not only between industries but sometimes within the same one. Men would be working in a particular area in one place and women in the same area in another. Yet in each case we would be told why men or women were particularly suited for the job—apparently the same job. What this brought home to us over and over again was the fact that there is nothing inherent in a job that makes it male or female. The gender definition of jobs, and sexual division of labour, are socially and historically constructed. A 'logic' to the organisation of work did emerge; but only once we began to think in terms of the dynamics of the gender construction: how masculinity and femininity are produced in *relation* to each other through work. Changes in the labour process are not only obscured by the sexual division of labour, they potentially disrupt its reproduction by provoking contradictions in the process of gender construction. We hope to show that the question of how management control might be challenged by the workforce is ultimately bound up with how the sexual division of labour might be confronted.

1 Masculinity and machines
Automation in manufacturing industry

Sir—The Minister for Employment and Youth Affairs, Mr Viner, has called on employers and developers to train more people in Australia to avoid skilled labour shortages in the 1980s ('The Advertiser' 2/12/80).

I am employed in the whitegoods industry and am a qualified spray painter, having had three years on-the-job experience in NZ and ten in the industrial field here in Australia.

Recently I spent nine months at the Croydon School of Further Education learning more about industrial painting, including electrostatic coating, powder coating etc. and three months on-the-job training on the Ransburg system.

Where I work the shop is now closing (because of a paint process being introduced by the steel manufacturers), and as far as I am concerned, it appears I will be transferred to unskilled labour, in which case all this training has just been a waste of time.

How many people will become unemployed after their training because of automation? I shall ask Mr Viner this question in the late 1980s. Bob Kramer, Dulwich. Letters to the Editor: *The Advertiser* (Adelaide).

Probably one day a robot will take over.

Today they need me, tomorrow they might not.

Machinery seems to be taking over.

The new computerised instrumentation is replacing us.

They are closing down too much of this plant and forcing people to leave.

I think this factory is going to close down soon.

Nobody is permanent today.

T HESE comments come from workers in the whitegoods industry. It is one of the industries in Australia which has so far *survived* the restructuring that is taking place in the manufacturing sector. This chapter is about the terms of survival, the costs to the workforce in terms of loss of jobs and skills, and the gender implications of these costs.

In the new international division of production there is little room for an independent viable manufacturing base in Australia. In this division,

Australia is being designated as a provider of energy, foodstuffs, and industrial raw materials; the US and Japan as sources of capital; and the Asian countries as providers of cheap labour and commodities. The effects of the present recession have been exacerbated by weaknesses in the structure of Australian manufacturing which developed in the postwar boom. Manufacturing was largely geared towards import substitution by means of high levels of protection. This enabled a large number of companies to operate on a small scale, often with out-of-date technology. Unable to compete, many of these firms have now gone out of business. Others, both foreign-owned and Australian, are locating their production facilities elsewhere, particularly in SE Asia. Those industries and firms which remain are rationalising their operations in an attempt to boost productivity and become more competitive. The most visible effect of this has been the massive loss of jobs in all manufacturing industries, whether through closing of plants or the introduction of capital-intensive equipment. For example, in the period 1974–79, 26,000 jobs disappeared in the clothing and footwear industries and 32,000 in the household appliances and electrical equipment industries (Department of Employment and Youth Affairs, 1979).

We chose the whitegoods industry for a case study from the manufacturing sector. Whitegoods falls in the middle of the spectrum of manufacturing industries: both foreign and local capital are involved; it has been neither capital nor labour intensive; and has not been either a 'male' or 'female' industry. While there is a wide range of jobs and skills in the industry, something like 70 per cent of the workforce are classified as semi-skilled and unskilled (Industries Assistance Commission, 1978: 10). The composition of the workforce is mixed. The large numbers of semi-skilled and unskilled jobs created with mass production were filled by migrant men and women and Australian women. Migrant workers made up 70 per cent of production workers in 1978 (Department of Industry and Commerce, 1978: 16) and in 1974 women were estimated to make up 60 per cent of the workforce in production areas (Department of Labour and Immigration, 1975: 9). The 'mix' of jobs and workers makes the whitegoods industry a particularly good case study for an analysis of the relationship between changes in the labour process and the assignment of tasks to particular sections of the workforce.

The structure of the whitegoods industry

In 1946 only 13 per cent of Australian homes had a refrigerator and a mere two per cent had a washing machine (Australian Women's Weekly, 1960: 12–24). By the 1970s these commodities had become almost universal, while a big proportion of households owned freezers and clothes dryers and a new market had opened for dishwashers and room air conditioners. The demand for new stoves more than kept pace with these items throughout the period.

The whitegoods industry mushroomed in the years immediately after World War II, in the context of the general expansion of manufacturing. It played an integral part in creating the appearance of prosperity and mobility associated with the expansion of consumption patterns, producing some of those products that were advertised as being essential to every Australian home. A large number of companies turned to whitegoods production with high tariff walls and the expectation of unlimited market growth. By 1953, no less than 35 firms were involved in making four leading products—refrigerators, freezers, washing machines and stoves (Department of Industry and Commerce, 1978: 3). Most manufacturers produced a complete range of products. Several companies set up whitegoods production via links with big US companies thus taking advantage of American technology and marketing. These are the companies that have survived into the 1970s.

By the late 1950s demand had slackened and, in the credit squeeze of 1960–61, about twenty companies left the industry or were taken over. In the late 1960s there was an upsurge in replacements as the purchases of the 1950s wore out, and there was a new demand for small refrigerators (especially with the motel boom), automatic washing machines, dryers and room air conditioners. But there was little further reduction in the number of companies.

The conditions of the seventies pushed the industry more quickly to rationalisation. With other industries, it has been the subject of numerous Tariff Board and IAC investigations. In 1973 the Federal government cut tariffs by 25 per cent across the board. Early in 1974, acting on a Tariff Board report, it began to introduce further tariff reductions in whitegoods to induce reorganisation on more economic lines. These events coincided with the onset of the recession in mid-1974 and an immediate drop in demand. The industry was hard hit by this and sackings followed.

There was a further IAC report on whitegoods in 1978 which the government quickly accepted. This confirmed the need for restructuring to reduce the number of producers and to allow those remaining to achieve production volumes and methods similar to major overseas manufacturers. This would enable them to take advantage of economies of scale and introduce more sophisticated technology. The government gave notice that tariff rates would be reduced over a six year period, thus giving the industry two years longer than the IAC had recommended. Both the IAC and the government evaded the question of the effects on employment.

In March 1979 a sharemarket battle took place between the major whitegoods companies in direct response to the government's decision. In less than three weeks three major ownership changes occurred.

Email took over Kelvinator; Simpson Pope took over Malleys; and Rank (a subsidiary of the British firm) and AGE (a subsidiary of US General Electric) formed two joint companies under the dominance of Rank. This meant the emergence of three major groups. The other two companies whose future in Australia is still uncertain are Philips (Dutch) and Hoover (UK). The two leaders, Simpson Pope and Email, have made agreements on product specialisation, and both are proceeding with rationalisation and technological innovation in order to increase productivity and profitability.

The sexual division of labour in mass production plants

The concept of skill was traditionally bound up with craft mastery. An overall knowledge of products and processes was combined with the manual dexterity required to actually carry on a specific branch of production. With mechanisation and mass production we have seen the decline of the all-round skilled tradesman and the development of a fragmented labour process. Tradesmen's skills were incorporated into the new machines, or concentrated into particular tasks. As work was simplified, there was a considerable growth in jobs for process workers and semi-skilled machine operators. Production was organised around a few specialist skilled jobs on the one hand, and a large number of semi-skilled and unskilled ones on the other. This involved a double-sided process of 'hyperskilling' and 'deskilling'. As mental labour was separated from manual labour, and control from execution, the concept of 'skill' was narrowed from an overall understanding of the production process to a highly specialised knowledge of a particular area. At the same time the majority of workers were treated as having no skills, or at most, limited skills.

Work in a typical whitegoods mass production plant is divided into three main areas:

1 Highly skilled areas not involved directly in production, but in the making and servicing of equipment, such as maintenance, tool room, electrical work.
2 Fabrication areas where components are made and processed. These areas are mixed in terms of level of skill.
3 Assembly and sub-assembly, which is predominantly 'unskilled' work.

Some of these areas are clearly segregated along sex lines, others are mixed. In both cases a sexual division of labour operates, although in the latter it is less immediately obvious. It is based on a series of polarities which are broadly equated with masculinity and femininity. The most obvious distinction is between skilled and unskilled work. The other main ones are: heavy/light, dangerous/less dangerous, dirty/clean, interesting/boring, mobile/immobile. The first of each of these pairs is held to be appropriate for men, or men are assumed to be better at it. The second is seen as appropriately 'female'. In the second case, nature is much more frequently invoked: women, 'by nature' are good at boring, fiddly and sedentary work. 'Men's work' does not seem to require the same rationalisation: presumably they have more power to say what they will and will not do. Thus, to this list we could add a further series of categories around congenial/uncongenial. Men may do the dirtier and more dangerous jobs but they are also able to exercise more control over their working conditions, over problems associated with heat, light, fresh air or draughts.

These polarities operate across the manufacturing sector as a whole. They not only define jobs within an industry or factory but across industries. Industries such as iron and steel are defined as 'male' because they are heavy or dangerous; others, like electronics, are defined as 'female' because they involve light, repetitive work. In industries which are predominantly male, for example, sugar refining (skilled, mobile and heavy work), women are concentrated in labour intensive assembly areas of packaging (repetitive, immobile, light). We turn now to look at these polarities in whitegoods in more detail.

Skilled/unskilled

Skilled work takes place in the first two areas referred to above. Toolmakers, fitters, die setters and electricians work in the making and servicing of tools and machinery. In the production areas too there are a number of jobs that require tradesmen's skills. First class machinists, first class sheetmetal workers and first class welders do precision work. They are involved in the setting up of machinery and following blueprints and plans. Together these workers constitute a hyper-skilled elite in relation to the rest of the workforce. Skilled work is done exclusively by males who are predominantly Anglo-Saxon and Northern European. The subdivision and fragmentation of metalwork meant an increase in semi-skilled jobs, involving the operation and sometimes setting up of machines. Some women are to be found in the ranks of the 'second' and 'third' class machinists. However, most are concentrated in unskilled process and assembly line jobs. Within these latter areas there is a further sex-typing of jobs. We must note here that what is defined as a 'skill' is heavily ideological and already biased towards men. Women's skills, especially if acquired informally, go unacknowledged.

Heavy/light

This is a well established distinction that is used quite consciously as a way of dividing jobs. It is formalised in the sense that there is legislation limiting the weights that can be lifted by women. Although the rationale of such legislation is to 'protect' women it is fairly clear that it in fact serves other purposes as well. In all-female industries such as clothing and textiles, women lift weights over the legal limit—in this case it suits management. In industries with both men and women the distinction operates to preserve men's jobs. In whitegoods it provides the rationale for a sexual division of labour in the areas where both men and women work, namely production and assembly. In fabrication and components areas men work on the heavier components—in the case of washing machines, hobs and base plates. In press shops, men work on large presses, women on small ones. Men do all the lifting of components and products. In one factory, though the majority of workers on a motor assembly line are women, men actually lift the compressors off at the end. In the same factory in the sealed units area, women put parts in, assemble heat exchanges and copper piping. We were told that this is 'light work that men won't do'. A very telling statement which implies that the distinction has less to do with the physical capabilities of women than with men's sense of what kind of work is appropriate for them.

Dangerous/less dangerous, dirty/clean

These operate in much the same way. Large presses are seen as more dangerous and dirty than small ones; foundries are both dirty and dangerous and pickling is a cleaning process that involves working with dangerous acids. This is therefore 'men's work'. Again the rationale is in terms of women's nature, in this case with specific reference to biology, the danger to reproductive capacities. It is, nonetheless, an arbitrary distinction: women in whitegoods factories are subjected to dangerous and unhealthy working conditions along with the other employees. And some of them do work in areas regarded as the most dirty and/or dangerous. Enamel shops, because of the heat and dust, are traditionally seen as a male area but in one factory were operated entirely by migrants—women as well as men. The sexual division of labour intersects with a division by ethnicity. Often 'migrant social networks' are used to recruit people for jobs that Australians are reluctant to do. In this way, some women become 'honorary men' without the workplace advantages which accrue to being a man. Similarly core-blowing machines, both dangerous and physically difficult to use, were operated entirely by migrant women. It would seem that the health of migrant women is given the lowest priority. Management, following the logic of profitability and control, 'simply' draws on sexual and ethnic divisions (combined in the idea that migrant women are not 'real women but workhorses). They are able to do this because workers themselves accept these divisions as inevitable, part of their lived reality. Some groups (men, Australians) have a clear short-term interest in preserving these divisions. This is obvious in the case of some of the tradesmen, who do not bother to conceal their contempt for production workers as almost subhuman, and who are for the most part concerned only with their own working conditions and pay differentials.

Interesting/boring

This relates to the broad distinction between skilled and unskilled work but also operates within mixed areas, production and assembly. Women do all the boring, repetitive work. Even on assembly lines where all work is basically this, distinctions are drawn—women do the most boring work. It is seen to be in women's nature to be able to tolerate boring, repetitive work; it is something they will put up with but men won't. Management will go so far as to claim that women prefer this type of work, partly because of the social interaction that they supposedly have with other women and partly because it requires little thought or effort. 'Women don't seem to have the same problem with boredom that men do.' More to the point, we were told that a vacuum cleaner assembly line was made up entirely of migrant women because 'it is too boring for men'. Yet in that same factory men worked on the washing machine line doing very similar work. The differences, then, can be very slight. But they are important to workers on the job and they serve to reassure men of their superiority, by distinguishing their work from 'women's work'. The distinction rests not on the inherent quality of the work but almost entirely on the meaning given to it in particular contexts.

Mobile/immobile

Unlike the earlier distinctions, this one is not used explicitly but it has a powerful, if hidden, effect in reproducing gender differences. The dichotomy can be understood in terms both of movement in the actual job and movement around the factory allowed by the job. All women's jobs are immobile with the exception of cleaning on the assembly line (clearly not a male job!). The die setters, maintenance workers and the forklift drivers are men, and their work involves movement around the factory. Occasionally a company will employ a women as a forklift driver to show that they don't discriminate but she will clearly be seen as an exception, treated by male workers as a danger or a joke—this being the range of male orthodoxy on women drivers. Tradesmen move freely around their machines, around the section or around the whole plant. They are the only ones likely to be familiar with its general layout. Electrical wiring, which must be one of the most tedious of jobs, is also the least mobile: it is done by women. Even in the 'mixed' areas the distinction operates. For example, work on large presses involves a lot more movement than that on smaller ones. On assembly lines men do the jobs requiring more movement—where there is more than one aspect to the operation or the heavier work on the larger appliances. Women do the work that is more minute, 'fiddly', requiring very little movement. This endorses men's need for a sense of freedom and mobility and reinforces the notion that women are passive and should not be free to move around. Space is controlled by men.

Comically, men see themselves as tigers pacing restlessly around on the outside, while women are settled serenely in the 'cave' (or the 'glass house' as the harness section at Email is called). Undoubtedly this access to space gives men greater control over their conditions of work, however trivial. A male press operator will feel free to stroll away from his machine and light a cigarette. The women press operators would not get away with it but would be expected to spend spare moments setting up their machines for the next round.

This sort of thing makes women workers very bitter. They see, in countless ways, that men have an easier time of it at work even though they ostensibly do the 'harder' more 'manly' jobs. Many of them said things had got worse since equal pay. A lot of the men seem to feel emasculated by 'mere' equality and insulted that women receive the same base rates. In this situation they attempt to reassert their patriarchal authority by expecting women to work harder than they do, in order, as they see it, to 'right the balance'.

The way the labour process is organised in manufacturing means that overall, work is deskilled and there is little control of the process on the part of the work force. However, some jobs allow for a greater sense of control than others—and these are performed by men. While men can construct for themselves a sense of superiority, they are less likely to buck the system. Indeed, the degradation of all work is obscured by the allocation of the most degraded jobs to women.

The process whereby male workers measure their jobs against the type of work that women do occurs across the manufacturing sector as a whole. Men doing unskilled jobs in an all male industry can compare their work with that in an all female industry. Of course in such a case it is likely to be migrants in the unskilled jobs and the main divisions and polarities operating internally would be ethnic ones. But the process of generating polarities based on minor overall differences is much the same.

Automation and changes in the sexual division of labour

The whitegoods industry is in a stage of transition following recent restructuring. Automation comes in as part of wider rationalisation processes including product specialisation (Email is concentrating on refrigerators, Simpson on washing machines), the use of precut, prepainted metal, the switch to components which are either imported or made elsewhere in Australia, the use of common components, and the subcontracting of some parts and processes. Although there is no neat distinction between mechanisation and automation, and the process of automation under way is an uneven one, the general trends are clear.

Automation involves not only the drastic reduction of labour but the introduction of new principles of control and decision-making. Technical control, whereby the control mechanism is designed into the machine, is taken a step further with self-regulation and feedback devices being built into automated machines. The function of machine operator is replaced by that of supervisor of machine systems. Thus to a large degree the previous combination of mental and manual skills is removed, and the skilled function is more a technical one of overseeing the whole system. There is a new division between a few 'skilled' technical workers, and unskilled quasi-technical operators.

Two sorts of computer based automation are being introduced: automatic transfer equipment (robots) and numerical control machines. Robots are being applied to operations such as welding, spray painting and moving materials from one machine to another. Each robot displaces perhaps three to five workers. They can work twenty-four hours a day without flagging and they don't put in workers' compensation claims. In one plant we visited a press had failed and come down on the arm of a robot. Management proudly told us that this was much cheaper to replace than a human arm! In addition, the use of robots can turn what had formerly been separate, individual job operations into a single, integrated, automatically controlled process.

Numerically controlled machines carry out a series of motions on the basis of a predetermined program. The semi-skilled functions of feeding in the work and inspecting that the job has been done properly are substantially reduced by inbuilt mechanisms for self-control and self-regulation. An operator is still required but does not operate the machine so much as mind/monitor it. Like the robots, these machines are flexible, for they can be reprogrammed for a variety of operations. They can be combined with robots to establish a continuous flow production process. Instead of parts being produced in batches with consequent delays and bottlenecks, more and more of the production process is being directly linked to the assembly line and many of the separate 'shops' will eventually disappear. At Simpson Pope a new gearbox line takes castings produced in the company's foundry in one end and turns out the finished gearbox at the other. Requiring only one operator, the new line has replaced 18 machines which previously worked three shifts a day. It can turn out a completed gear box every 40 seconds.

Numerical control makes it possible to remove calculation and judgment from skilled machinists on the shop floor, and place it in the hands of programmers. With these forms of automation the double-sided process of deskilling and hyperskilling is taken a step further. But again we have to remember that the definition of skill is highly political. In a situation where work is changing rapidly, the struggle for new skills to be recognised is of central importance and we cannot afford to stay with the conventional but outdated definitions. In an effort to maintain and raise wage rates, the AMWSU has thus argued for reskilling before industrial tribunals.

With automation changes in the nature of work are accompanied by a reorganisation of the sexual division of labour. As this is a period of transition, we are talking about trends that are becoming discernable rather than patterns that are already firmly established. In terms of the dichotomies outlined above, the following trends can be observed:

1 Overall there is a narrowing in the range of skills involved. In the highly skilled areas jobs are being reduced and deskilled.
2 The work is less heavy and involves less lifting. This results partly from the introduction of lighter materials such as plastics and partly from automation, in particular automatic transfer equipment and changes in materials handling. Overhead conveyors are used to move products and components from one section of the plant to another and in some cases from one building to another.
3 Work is less dangerous and less dirty in the traditional sense. For example, automated presses and robots eliminate dangerous jobs in press work. This needs qualification. Management introduce robots not for humanitarian reasons but to save labour and reduce compensation costs. There are also new health risks associated with automation. These result from the use of new materials such as plastics and certain gases, the greater use of shiftwork to keep the new expensive machinery in continuous operation and a speeding up of the production process with the implementation of flow line principles. Increased pressure of work was a constant refrain in every factory we visited.
4 Work is more boring and routine than ever, involving a lot more machine-minding and pushing of buttons. The new technology not only displaces labour but it removes companions. One person works with a series of robots rather than with other people.
5 There is overall less mobility, with people's movements being controlled by automated machinery.

What these changes in the nature of work amount to is the erosion of the basis of the established sexual division of labour. All jobs are becoming more like women's jobs, as they have traditionally been defined. What we will see, however, is that this has not led to a breakdown in the sexual division of labour as might be expected once the distinctions between male and female jobs lose significance. In fact the division of labour is being reproduced along different lines and is an integral part of the reorganisation of work. One of the consequences is that men are now doing jobs that previously would have been done by women. These can be redefined as male, because the jobs done predominantly or exclusively by women have in some ways got worse. Women are now concentrated in fewer jobs than previously and these are in the remaining labour intensive areas that are likely to be automated in the future. Taking each area in turn we will outline the changes under way.

Highly skilled areas

Changes in the labour process have not led to changes in the sexual division of labour. These are traditional male areas, and remain so. Overall numbers have been reduced and management are attempting to replace traditional specialists, such as fitters, with tradesmen who have 'adaptability and versatility'. In other circumstances this might have been followed by an influx of women. But in a situation of high unemployment the men want to hang on to these jobs which are still preferable to others likely to be available in the factory or elsewhere. Moreover their incumbents remain the most highly organised and relatively privileged section of whitegoods workers.

Production areas

Work in press shops has been reduced as a result of the move from metal to plastics and with increased automation. Thus jobs overall have gone but more women's jobs have gone than men's. Men always predominated on the large presses but there were many more women working on them than there are now. This is despite the fact that the work is lighter and could thus be seen as more appropriate for women. Women once predominated on the small presses but now are a minority. We were told at Email that women are afraid of the presses! This the women denied vigorously, recalling earlier days. In the less automated press shops women still work the small old presses. When Kelvinator brought in new presses (where the large/small distinction has little relevance) it attempted to remove all women from the area. The company asserts that women make more compensation claims—a claim which the workers reject. One of the women displaced has taken her case to the Commissioner for Equal Opportunity. Kelvinator responded by investigating the possibility of applying for an exemption under the South Australian Sex Discrimination Act. This makes discrimination on the grounds of sex lawful when sex is a 'genuine occupational qualification'. When Kelvinator realised they were unlikely to win such a case, they proceeded to deny that the Act applied to the situation, since they work under a federal award. They are currently planning to go to the Federal Arbitration Court to establish that the work is unsuitable for women. And so the fight goes on. Unfortunately the Act does not allow for class actions. Judgments apply only to the instigators, who cannot act on behalf of the whole category of people affected. Whatever the company's rationalisations, the move can be seen as part of a process of constituting a whole area of work as 'male' as the jobs have been reduced. At Kelvinator the numbers in the press shop have dwindled for 120 to little more than 30. Ironically there is less physical effort required than before—the work has been reduced to pushing a button. Yet this gives 'power' over complex machinery and is thus seen to be a male preserve.

Similarly, women have been pushed out of welding where they have maintained a minority presence since the war. The film *Rosie the Riveter* shows how women were encouraged to do this work and then kicked out into lower paid 'women's work' when the servicemen came home. Only a few managed to stay in the area and now their jobs are threatened. In one factory we were told that they didn't like the work. The women said that it was 'yucky' but insisted that they were perfectly capable of doing it and felt angry about attempts to push them out. In another factory, with the introduction of a machine that combines spot and seam welding, management attempted to remove a woman who had been doing welding for 20 years and replace her with the male leading hand. The argument was that women don't understand machines as well. The job was being deskilled and yet a woman was being removed from it.

There seems to be a considerable mystification of machines, despite the fact that operating them is very simple. This touches on a general pattern that is emerging. Work becomes simplified with automation, and yet it is men minding the machines—the rationale being that women don't understand them or are frightened of them. Thus a new distinction is being set up between technical/non-technical jobs. If women worked on these machines it would be clear that the work involved stationary and repetitive tasks. With men on the machines, rather than women, the further loss of control of the work process is disguised. Male workers are able to represent the power of the machine as theirs and experience themselves as having 'technical' expertise. They can then measure their jobs against women's non-technical jobs. The machine symbolises masculinity and enables them to live out fantasies about power and domination which in turn reproduce this connection. Their situation is very similar to that of computer operators, as we show in a later chapter when we talk about the computer as phallus.

The distinction between technical and non-technical carries over into other areas as well. In plastics, men are involved in making the doors and liners while women produce the smaller components. The rationale given here is not size but the form of technology; the machines making doors and liners are thought to require more 'technical' skill. It may seem anomalous that women mind even the smaller machines but plastics manufacture is a new process, automated from the beginning and not replacing a previous process that required skill or allowed for some control. We may note in passing that the increased use of plastics has contributed to reductions in areas like the paint shop and enamelling. These remain 'male' domains but the numbers of workers in them have declined drastically. This in turn creates pressure to change some of the female jobs to male jobs. There are two assumptions being made here. First, that men have a prior right to employment. And secondly, that they should not have to do 'women's work' and that the job description should correspond to masculinity as a superior way of being. Women are increasingly concentrated in the production of motors and harnesses. This is a labour intensive area, requiring dexterity and concentration. It is also tedious work that is acknowledged to cause tenosynovitis (though one manager took biology further than usual in insisting that 'women had weaker wrists'). The making of harnesses is still highly manual, with workers having to thread wires around a frame—a simple and repetitive process requiring lots of quick hand movements. Management tried to convince us that, in these otherwise unpleasant jobs, women liked the company of other women. Yet they were so tied to one spot, and the pace of work so fast, that they scarcely had time to say hello to each other.

Assembly

It was assembly and sub-assembly that opened up jobs for women and migrants in the postwar period of mass production. Though men and women work 'side by side' the polarities are as present here as anywhere else, though there is less of a general pattern. Usually lines are predominantly male or predominantly female. There are two further factors determining workforce composition: labour supply and the requirements of short-/long-term workforce. When a long-term stable workforce was required, married women were used. With current uncertainties in the industry, and fluctuating labour needs, there seems to have been some preference for young men, who are perceived as more mobile. For once, it is a male workforce which supplies 'natural' wastage. These young men will not put up with poor working conditions and tend to move on. The women know they will be unlikely to do better elsewhere even if they could find another job (Jacka and Pringle, 1981: 12–17).

In one case when women were being moved off a line, the explanation management gave for the all-male workforce was that 'women wouldn't want to work closely with men'. This is a fairly common view, expressed by the workers themselves and it contains a thinly-veiled reference to the threat of sexual harassment which men hold over women, whether or not they implement it. Where these sorts of considerations affect the distribution of men and women on the line the proportion of different migrant groups depends to a large extent on the labour supply in the particular area. Email Orange is exceptional in having no Southern European migrants in the workforce. Factories in Sydney have employed people from each successive migration wave to take the dirtiest jobs: Italians, Greeks, Yugoslavs, Turks, Lebanese, Chileans and now Vietnamese.

Assembly and sub-assembly are still labour-intensive but here too changes in manufacture have brought a reduction in the number of jobs. The indications are that they will become more closely integrated with production as the whole becomes a flow process. As it becomes a viable proposition management will replace people with robots on the assembly line. Women and migrants are likely to bear the brunt of continuing job losses.

Demystifying machines

In whitegoods, changes in the nature of work which result from automation have undermined the basis of the sexual division of labour established in the period of mass production and mechanisation. There is a progressive loss of skills, particularly the combination of mental/manual that defined skilled male work, and all work becomes increasingly like what was previously defined as female. This has led neither to an end of sex-typing nor to the expulsion of men from the industry. Rather it is men who do the newly-created deskilled jobs, mainly involving operating/minding machines. Many more women are losing employment with the big decline in unskilled jobs and those left are further concentrated in the remaining labour intensive assembly line areas, doing the most menial, repetitive work. Thus a sexual division of labour continues on the basis of the new dichotomies of technical/non-technical associated with changes in work. An association has been made between technology and masculinity which continues to obscure the extent of deskilling and loss of jobs.

What happens with automation in all-male industries where the sexual division of labour does not operate as such an immediate mechanism of control? In no cases are women employed in the new deskilled jobs. Tooth's Breweries has just spent $80 million setting up completely new fully-automated plants. Redundancy agreements were negotiated and the workforce almost completely replaced. They claim to be having difficultly recruiting men to operate the new plants and are surprised because 'the same skills are required, except of course manual ones'. The nature of the work is qualitatively different—a controller stands in a control room looking at a board of switches and knobs—no beer is actually sighted. There has been no attempt to recruit women to these jobs. However, it is perhaps no coincidence that for the first time, Tooths have begun to employ women in what is usually a female area—packaging lines. Will this make a plant operator's job more palatable? Will he feel more manly if what he is doing is thus clearly distinguished from women's work?

In whitegoods, as in many other manufacturing industries, automation is introduced in a piecemeal way and skilled workers are often put on the new machines during the debugging phase or until they retire, in order to prevent disputes. Where automation takes place suddenly there is likely to be open conflict. Tradesmen in whitegoods and other industries are now becoming concerned about threats to job security and job satisfaction posed by technological change. Yet it is very much their own job security and satisfaction; it is one of the consequences of hyperskilling that tradesmen are removed from the main areas of production and have little concern for the interests of workers there.

One of our basic propositions is that one way in which management can get people to work is via gender identity. Deskilling is a potential threat to masculinity. We have shown how in whitegoods this identity is retained by the men remaining in the industry because they have been able to measure their work against women's work. Thus not only management but male workers have derived benefits (albeit short-term) from a sexual division of labour and are involved in the recreation of these divisions.

However, telling it like this simplifies the story. It suggests that there is no struggle over either changes in the labour process or changes in the sexual division of labour. Clearly there are examples of men being conscious of and resisting changes in their work. What is not so readily recognised is the way in which women resist this process. In the whitegoods industry the most significant shift in the sexual division of labour has involved moving women off machines and their replacement by male operators. The justifying ideology has been that women are scared of, or don't understand, machines. This new sexual division of labour has been established with appeals to the 'natural' qualities of women and yet these women are only too well aware of their capabilities with operating machines.

Women are resisting attempts to move them off machines. In the press shop at Kelvinator some of the women are fighting management's attempts to turn the shop into a male area. They take pride in their work and are extremely angry about the way they have been treated: 'They're two-faced mongrels. They can't do without us, yet we're not good enough for them'. That a case has been taken up with the Commissioner for Equal Opportunity in South Australia suggests a developing consciousness of sexual discrimination.

This suggests that the construction of femininity in relation to work is very much a contradictory process. Women do not just see themselves as wives and mothers and placidly accept whatever happens to them in the work situation. *The Survey of Workers in the Whitegoods Industry* (Jacka & Pringle, 1981) found evidence to suggest that women who had worked in the industry on a long-term basis were more conscious of changes and the effects of technology than men. Many of the men in the process work areas see their jobs as short-term, and a high proportion of men are sole breadwinners. Consequently they are most concerned with their own immediate short-term interests.

> The young Australian males are the hardest to organise because they don't expect to be there long. They're individualists and sit around talking about booze, sport, chicks, but no one's allowed to 'talk politics'. If they're buying a house they're easier to organise—then they can see the point. (Kelvinator shop steward)

The women, (frequently in a two-income household) expressed a keener sense of injustice and a willingness to pursue not only their self-interest but the interests of workers as a whole. They are amongst the most active and knowledgeable of the shop stewards. This contradicts the union stereotype that the presence of women in an industry makes it difficult to organise. Unions would be well advised to take note of this and encourage the involvement of women in organising struggles to protect jobs, wages and working conditions in industries such as whitegoods. Their differences from the men are not necessarily a weakness (as male unionists often arrogantly assume) but a source of strength. They are likely to have a clearer and more integrated perspective on the kinds of changes that are needed.

2 Kentucky-fried money
The banks

IN February 1982 a personnel manager in one of Australia's most conservative banks organised a 'women at work' get-together of eight 'career' women, to which we were invited. Three years earlier, when we began research on the banks, we experienced considerable difficulty getting interviews with people in this bank. Now there is a change of image: the bank provides job and career opportunities for women.

Well, what has changed, and why? Here is what these women had to say on the position of women in banks:

> As a matter of fact my first appointment was as manager's assistant. I had to go and ask for it because I was dealing with managers and accountants and had no status whatever and, I thought, this is wrong. I took the view that if you got a good report you were considered as such . . . then I realised that the banks were so conservative at that time [early 1970s] that you had to get off your bottom and do it yourself. I then received a managerial appointment. . . . Previously they always had a male to come in and do the job . . . and I had to more or less do it for him and advise him . . . with industrial work you had to know all the awards and he of course just didn't know it . . . that happened right through my career and I'm sure it happened to the other girls here. . . . When I was in the ledger department, supervisors used to come in when I was examiner and they'd ring my desk and say, teach them what goes on down here . . . and the next thing I knew they'd be my supervisor. But that was something we accepted . . . I think we were brainwashed . . . in my time that's what happened. The girls thought that if you had a good report you'd be looked after—that was not the case.
> (Manager, Services Staff Administration; has been with the bank 33 years)

> There is some stage where you say, no more . . . are you going to train the next person to be your supervisor . . . I think you do come to that stage where you have that discussion with your accountant one afternoon. . . . For all the publicity, you still have to ask for promotion and there's a lot of nepotism.
> (Manager's Assistant)

> I had to write a stinking letter to personnel to get out [of examining], and was classified as a stirrer. I came up against a bit of hostility. I became a general hand and was in charge of the tellers . . . and the first teller wouldn't speak to me because he had wanted that job and the accountant wouldn't speak to me because he had wanted a male. . . . The bank's got their tuppence worth out of me . . . (Senior Research Officer)

I've never asked for it ... been in the bank 20 years ... appointed in 1975.... In staff training for twelve months before I was appointed as a senior instructor ... I instructed induction courses right through to accountant before that. (Accountant)

I think it's going to get more difficult. There were a few years when they thought they had to [promote women] because of equal rights. It'll slow down after accountant level. There are already guys who've done advanced management training. They've been promised jobs but there just aren't the jobs there for them. There's guys around now who are in their forties and haven't got manager's jobs. (Accountant)

Male recruitment?

It's a banking image problem—the males think, well there's not going to be enough careers, so why bother, there's no incentive ... if people still think of a male as a breadwinner. (Assistant to Manager)

People get accustomed to the change ... they no longer comment on a female accountant and they're mostly surprised to see a male teller these days. (Accountant)

Mobility

What irks me is that I was never *asked* if I wanted to go anywhere. The guys were asked if they wanted to go to New Guinea. When I approached my boss he said, you wouldn't want to go anywhere, you'd want to stay here.... And I said, well until you ask me you don't know... So I'll wait and see whether he does. I didn't want to go to New Guinea anyway ... but it worries me, other people are going past you. (Senior Research Officer)

Cash shops

That's an area be well out of. That is where they'll shunt women.... They'll say, oh yes you're a bank manager ... you'll only be able to lend up to $15,000 which won't even buy a house ... (Manager's Assistant)

All the managers are a little worried because they're not going to go anywhere ... so if they're not going anywhere what chances have we got of going? (Accountant)

These women spoke openly about discrimination, and were cynical about the opportunities for women when career opportunities for men are so limited. They, along with many other women we spoke to, see bank work as women's work now, precisely because of the lack of careers.

Banking provides a good case study of the relation between 'feminisation' and the process that is often conceptualised as 'proletarianisation' of the workforce. Sociologists have argued that feminisation acts as a counter to proletarianisation and provides the basis of separation between blue collar and clerical occupations (Giddens, 1973; Edwards,

1979; West, 1978). Such claims need to be looked at critically. To argue that clerical workers fail to develop working class consciousness because they are women is simplistic and sexist.

Banking does not fit neatly into the accounts, by Braverman and subsequent sociologists, of the similarities between the office and the factory and the transformation of the all-round clerical worker into a subdivided detail worker (Braverman, 1974; Nakano Glenn & Feldberg, 1979; de Kadt, 1979). Until very recently it has continued to be viewed as an area of predominantly mental labour providing middle-class careers. However, since World War II there have been continuous changes in the way bank work is organised and in the composition of the workforce. Technological change has increased the proportion of repetitive, routinised jobs and affected the career structure and employment opportunities. Women have moved from being a small proportion of bank staff (22.5 per cent in 1950) to about half (46.3 per cent in 1978). Banking is now dominated by very young workers, with one-third being under 21, and the majority under 27.

Technological change in the banking industry

The finance sector expanded rapidly in the postwar boom years. The mass production of goods had to be financed and so did the mass consumption of them. The extension of consumer credit facilities and the growth of hire purchase made it possible for the working class to acquire cars and a wide range of consumer durables such as refrigerators and washing machines. Home ownership increased by 15 per cent between 1947 and 1954 to reach 63 per cent in Australia as a whole (Kemeny, 1977: 83). By 1966 it had risen to 72 per cent though it declined thereafter (Australian Institute of Urban Studies, 1975: 7). The banks opened up new branches to cater for a growing population and new demands on the services. The expansion of savings and cheque accounts far exceeded population growth. On top of this the services became much more varied as the private banks moved into the savings field after 1956 as well as into hire purchase and unit trusts. This was followed by such things as travel departments, the extension of personal loans and, by the 1970s, Bankcard. In order to compete with other financial institutions the banks set up their own finance companies and took shares in (largely foreign-owned) merchant banks.

The bread and butter of banking is the processing of savings and current accounts. This is both labour intensive and the least profitable area of operations. The banks have a lot of capital and a vast workforce tied up in the branches while their main profits are coming from funds management, company accounts, and foreign exchange dealings. They have thus had every motivation to make labour more efficient and reduce costs. Mechanisation in the banks began with the introduction of ledger machines in the 1950s and proof machines in the 1960s but it was computerisation in the late 1960s that led to drastic changes in the labour process. Almost overnight it made ledger machinists and exchange clerks ancient history, centralising these functions in the electronic data processing (EDP) centres. By the early 1970s all the major savings and trading banks in Australia had established EDP centres, with the result that much of the work previously performed in branches is now centralised. Most branches in the main capital cities are now in networks linked to the computer centres and, apart from smaller branches which are still off-line (not directly connected to the computer), the majority are now on-line. This has meant a drastic rationalsation and reorganisation of the work process and the staffing arrangements in branches. The labour-saving effect has been massive.

Before computerisation each branch in a bank ran its own ledger system; different machines and systems were frequently used from one branch to another. With computerisation there is one set of programs; all accounting for all branches is dealt with centrally; calculation of fees, records of accounts and other such work has been removed from the branches. This represents a loss of autonomy for branches. Electronic machines and computer terminals in branches now record and transmit information which is processed and stored in the computer centre. Depending on the specific bank's system and level of automation, some processing takes place within branches. However, the back office work has been drastically reduced as information is punched into the terminals.

A number of stages in the labour process are now combined or reduced with this form of automation. Electronic machines both process work and record it. Proofing machines prove trading bank work, sort it and encode it. Prior to the introduction of these machines tellers proved their own work. Cheques are no longer posted in a ledger in the branch on which they were drawn but simply returned with a computer print out, the information having been centrally recorded. In the case of savings bank work, back office work is reduced as the teller uses the terminal to check the balance in the account.

The full potential of computerisation is now becoming clear, with area banking, automated telling, electronic funds transfer systems and the decline of branch banking becoming a reality. These changes are taking place in the context of the current rationalisation of the banking industry. Following the recent mergers/takeovers there are now only three major private banks in Australia. The Bank of Adelaide merged with the ANZ in 1979 after the collapse of its subsidiary the Finance Corporation of Australia Ltd. In 1981 the CBA was taken over by the Bank of NSW (which has now changed its name to Westpac) and the National merged with the CBC. In the aftermath of the Campbell report the finance sector as a whole is experiencing a major shake up: building societies and insurance companies are also merging.

Banks have been at a competitive disadvantage in relation to other financial institutions because of the labour costs associated with retail operations (branch networks) and government controls, particularly with regard to lending. With deregulation, recommended by Campbell, the shift into the wholesale area of corporate lending and foreign exchange and out of retail will be hastened. If social relations of work are sexualised, so also is the language of capital; as the *Australian Financial Review* put it, 'Although the marriage has already taken place, the wedding night is not until October, 1982.' (13 October 1981). The two recent 'marriages' will facilitate rationalisation of the branch networks: they can now be cut by half. Branch networks are also being reorganised with the introduction of area banking. The ANZ opened its first area branch in 1975 and now the Commonwealth and other private banks are moving into it. In each major area there is one large branch, with several smaller ones around it, but the bulk of the work, company accounts and major lending, is handled in the area branch. This amounts to a further downgrading of branches and of the status of many branch managers who will be little more than glorified supervisors. The new branches are called service centres or cash shops: 'piggy banks with junior managers'. When these are established, batching, that is the machining work now done in branches, will probably be centralised in a 'factory' in each area. It is claimed that the increased volume could 'save' four or five staff per branch. These changes will have severe effects on the workforce and it is not just junior staff who will bear the brunt: managers and people in head office are anxious about their futures also. Computerised systems like EFTS and automated tellers have less to do with 'convenient customer service' than efficient transfer of funds and rationalisation of branch work. Bank service is declining as rapidly as interest rates are rising.

Banking has always been seen as a career industry. The career structure is pyramid-shaped and very broad-based. The vast majority of staff are recruited at school-leaving age and may work their way up the pyramid through in-service training courses and good annual reports. The banks have always had a policy of 'growing their own' supervisory and managerial staff. Thus it is theoretically possible to start as messenger boy and work your way up to managing director. (No one ever speaks of messenger girls.)

Bank workers are not paid according to skill but according to age and sex. As with all clerical and administrative work, there have never been the clear skill differentials that exist in manufacturing industry and are associated with manual work. In contrast the 'mental' labour associated with white collar work has enabled bank employees to experience themselves as middle class. In fact, the majority of bank workers have probably always been part of the working class or close to it. The 'mental' labour of most bank clerks is minimal.

A pyramid, by definition, excludes most from the higher levels. What is significant about career structures in white-collar work is the ideology that attaches to them, that everyone has the opportunity to move into the ranks of management. This operates as a powerful means of control of the workforce. Bank work held out the possibility of upward mobility for the children of the lower middle class, especially in rural areas, and some sections of the working class. Such people were likely to be much more closely aligned with management ideologically than was the case in manufacturing. And it was precisely the middle class virtues of respectability, hard work, thrift, and sobriety that had to be cultivated if the transition were to be made. Bank workers handle money which symbolises an ultimate and objective measure of efficiency.

This system had considerable advantages for the banks. Everyone was assumed to be motivated towards achieving promotion and even today bank people talk about the importance of keeping up with their peers. It was easy to shift people around to any type of work without demarcation disputes or skill differentials to consider. This has made it relatively easy to introduce labour-saving technology and rationalisation of the labour process based on the advice of efficiency experts and work value studies.

But we have told only half the story. The career structure, which enabled banking to be treated as an avenue to secure, if not lavish, middle classness, applied to men only. Until the late 1960s women were obliged to resign from the permanent staff upon marriage. Until 1975 there were quite separate classification scales for men and women. Women were paid considerably less and were not eligible for the career grades. The career pyramid depended increasingly on the fact that much of the most menial work could be classified separately, and thus be lower paid, because it was being done by women.

Feminisation and the labour process

Women moved into the banks during World War II (24.4 per cent of the workforce in 1945) when they became ledgerkeepers and relief tellers. After the war they stayed because from the early 1950s onwards ledgerkeeping became mechanised and women were seen as more suitable to operate the machines. Ledgerkeeping was once the place where the majority of male clerks started off their careers. Machines were first introduced at some head offices and city branches in the 1930s. They were extended to other city and some suburban branches in the early 1950s and then became general. The first machines prepared statements and were used in conjunction with manually posted ledgers. Men and women thus worked side-by-side, men doing the hand posting and women operating the machines. In the 1960s these processes came together. The Dual Post System could be adjusted to post either ledger or statement sheets and the side-by-side system, though slower, could post the statement and ledger sheets simultaneously. The result of this was to halve the number of staff involved and to feminise the area. Women were using adding machines to balance up transactions, deposit child endowment payments, close accounts, handle transfer accounts, lost passbooks, and register signatures at other branches.

Women were thus moving into more central areas of banking, albeit at the lowest levels, but the ideology still prevailed that they were not really part of the bank. The ledger machinists were deliberately kept 'out of the firing line', ostensibly away from customers, in reality away from the wider activities of the bank, so that they could work harder. They were located at the back of the bank, face to the wall, working under conditions that the male clerks would not have tolerated. Thus productivity was increased not only by mechanisation but by the way work was organised.

Up to the mid 1960s the movement of women into the banks was directly related to mechanisation. They operated ledger and proof machines, taking over the most menial and lowest paid jobs. That this represented qualitative changes in the nature of bank work was disguised by the fact that it was being done by women.

In the period since 1965 major changes have taken place. The banks dropped their marriage bars and slowly opened up their career positions to women. Although the separate male and female classifications were retained, 'selected duties' schemes enabled some women to undertake telling and examining duties, though they were not allowed to progress any further. They were paid the male rates while they were doing these jobs but only after union pressure. This still did not amount to the full margins because the banks argued that although they were doing the same work as male examiners the males were younger and the appropriate scale was thus the male age scale adjusted downwards three years! The union refers to this as the 'three wise monkey's decision' in honour of the three members of the Full Bench. In addition, this 'promotion' was still along the women's line and thus constituted no challenge to the male career structure. At about the same time provision was made for a tiny minority of women to advance to senior supervisory positions. In the Commonwealth Bank this was known as the 'Women's Advanced Appointments Scheme', which took one batch of 30 women in 1968, its first year of operation. Similar schemes were set up in the other banks but the numbers likewise remained small. Following the 'equal pay for work of equal value' case in 1972, opportunities for women widened slightly. By the end of 1974, more than half of the women in banks, mainly 'junior' staff, were officially on equal pay though the discriminatory pay structure was not dismantled until 1975, following arbitration proceedings to enforce full equal pay. At that stage these two schemes were dropped and women were moved into the general classification.

As it stands at the moment, women have formal equality of opportunity: there is one general classification for men and women. In the specially classified grades there are still distinctions between keyboard and supervisory/managerial positions. These are not based on sex as such (though no men have as yet been appointed to the keyboard area!) and it is possible for people to move across from keyboard to supervisory levels.

A concern with sexual equality was not what motivated the banks to bring in these changes. Certainly the rising proportion of women employees did make it likely that pressure would be brought to bear. There was considerable bitterness amongst many of the senior women who often had responsibility for large numbers of staff, yet they suffered the indignity of seeing young boys paid more than they were and shooting up rapidly through the career grades. These women began to organise and to apply for male jobs for which they regarded themselves as qualified, in order to draw attention to the injustice. In the Commonwealth Bank they set up a Women's Advisory Council (WAC) which worked closely with the Commonwealth Bank Officers' Association (CBOA), in preparing cases for the Arbitration Commission. Female militancy coincided with the emergence for the first time of more general union militancy over pay and conditions. Yet the banks were curiously unmoved by this. The Commonwealth Bank claimed to have been little influenced by the WAC which merely 'let the girls think they had an outlet'. Presumably the numbers concerned were so small, approaches so timid, and organisation so limited, that the banks saw no serious threat to industrial relations.

Industrial legislation in the field of equal pay was only one of the factors, and not the most important, which determined bank policy on female employment. With equal pay the banks naturally moved women into previously male areas in order to 'get their money's worth' out of them, but, well before this, bank policies were changing in ways that would be hailed, retrospectively, as having 'anticipated' equal pay. In the first place, by the late 1960s, the banks were faced with practical difficulties in filling the telling line. In an expansionary period the occupation of bank clerk was becoming a less attractive choice for young men. On top of this, the proportion of the workforce under 20, from which the banks drew their staff, was declining. It was 13.7 per cent in 1966 and 11 per cent ten years later. The increase in university enrolments during this period meant a further decline in the number of young men available while the proportion of married women in the workforce was increasing. There was thus a relative shortage of males and an abundance of females. By putting women on the counter and paying them the full margin the banks could take on as married women, 'girls' they had previously trained.

Secondly, there was a desire to restrict male recruitment to longer-term executive needs. By this time the rate of expansion of branches was declining and a lot of labour-intensive work was disappearing. It could be anticipated that there would be less need for the supervisory positions to which men had traditionally been promoted. Thus a conscious decision was taken to change the mix of short-term and long-term career staff. Women have a very high drop-out rate and the banks can quite confidently predict how many will leave after four or five years. Most leave to have children by about age 25. While increasing numbers are making it to junior supervisory positions the number who go much further tapers off quite dramatically. Most have dropped out by the age 30. Natural wastage thus sorts out the problem of promoting large numbers to low level management.

The women who make it

Although very few women make it into management, some reach senior positions. These are predominantly older women who have worked in the banks for many years. The larger proportion of women in the bank workforce has also resulted in some making it into junior 'management'. Much the same process has occurred in retailing, as we show in the next chapter. A consideration of some representative cases shows how these women have 'slipped through' the types of obstacles faced by most.

Section officer in a savings bank

A softly spoken woman in her late fifties, Jane is perhaps the most senior woman in administration. She is highly competent but has not been one to push herself. She conceded that she was emotionally discomforted by having to be an equal with men, though intellectually she approved. Jane joined the bank following business college in 1940. When the men came back from the war she was relieved to 'go back to being a lady again'. She was promoted to manager's typist and enjoyed his kindly protection. 'It was like a family in the branches. I was well looked after ... the manager's wife taught me to drive'. After nine years, Jane was moved to the women's section, Staff Department, which was responsible for women's recruitment, annual reports, probationers' reports and troublesome people. Because she enjoyed this work, she didn't move into the advanced appointments scheme until 1969, twelve months after it had been introduced. She felt it was like 'being approved to be a man' but eventually did take up an appointment in the savings bank head office.

Jane lives alone, and has never married, a matter of some regret. She thinks the married girls have it really sewn up. They can combine work with stimulation at home and they have no financial worries; 'I don't mean the one's with children'. She has a lot of women friends in the bank who, like herself, are single. 'We were all born too early.... It was gloves and hat when I started, but now things have changed a lot and women are more accepted'. Somewhat ruefully she commented:

> Some women are able to be one of the boys. I haven't done that, I've made it without doing that ... I'm not ambitious ... I always waited to see where the bank put me ... I have to admit I miss my boss.

Branch manager

Elizabeth learned a lot about loans work as a result of many years as a loans manager's secretary. She was thus able to circumvent the usual difficulties women have in getting this kind of experience and eventually became an assistant loans manager. From that she moved to her current position. As a manager she is proud of her lending abilities—lending had gone up since she has been at the branch and she has good relations with local businesses. Many people, especially women, are glad to see a lady manager. Her solidly middle class background and manner are in contrast to the working class origins of many of the others. It puts her at ease in talking to customers and in handling such matters as property evaluations. Her style is quietly authoritative, while at the same time she takes care to make the men around her feel secure. 'It is up to the women to use tact and discretion over promotion. You can't come in with hobnailed boots. Some have, and have ruined their images'.

Elizabeth has never married, and has maintained close relationships with her family, living with them, and looking after them in illness. But her two worlds are kept quite separate.

Ex-branch manager

Robyn grew up in a country town and did a secretarial course when she left school. The branch manager was a family friend so the bank seemed a suitable place for her. This was 1945. After her application had been accepted management said they were sorry they'd taken her on because the boys were coming back and would need jobs. She was told to regard herself as a temporary. She is still there.

Robyn started as a junior, then progressed to typing with some ledger work, both pre- and post-ledger machines. As a typist she gained a lot of experience. Managers and accountants came to rely on her for information as to how the branch operated and about the bank's clientele. She took on a number of relieving positions before being appointed general hand but it was 27 years before she was regarded as a 'reasonable risk' to be promoted to accountant, assistant manager, and eventually manager of a prestigious city branch dealing mainly with business people. She has since been transferred to head office where she manages a contributory mortgage investment scheme. She misses the customer contact of branch work, but rationalises that: 'with machines you don't get it anyway'. The reason for her transfer is not clear, but on the face of it it looks like an example of a woman being 'kicked upstairs'. She thinks that the bank is no longer appointing women as branch managers.

These three women are typical of the old school. They did not have careers in mind when they first joined the bank. It was taken for granted that they would work until marriage and they then just 'stuck around for a long time'. All the women in senior positions we spoke to have either remained single or married late in life thus escaping the marriage bar. As typists and secretaries to men in senior positions they gained experience and knowledge, which helped them move once the career ladder was opened to women. Many grew up in the country where banking was one of the few prestigious, respectable jobs available:

> It was acceptable to my parents who would otherwise have kept me at home being a lady. (A branch manager)

What these women have to say about making it in a man's world is also interesting. They all think that women have to be careful not to push themselves too much, or they will ruin their images. Men will be threatened by women who do not retain their femininity. The section officer who felt that the bank was 'like a family' and now 'misses her boss' is a lovely example of the success of the banks' paternalistic form of control. On the other hand, most younger women prefer the more bureaucratic forms of control which have replaced this. A woman who is now an officer-in-charge in EDP and ten years younger than Jane had this to say:

> You can see what you are working towards, and given some luck, being in the right place at the right time, you will get there. You can use the bureaucratic structure, it is less chancy. You can also see your own assessments, and have more chance of making a realistic assessment of your own capabilities. I don't think there is much discrimination in EDP. If you have ability they're quite happy to exploit it, whatever your sex. So you have to take the bit by the teeth and see how you can make the most of it for yourself too.

Another group of senior women in banks are young technocrats who have not made their way up through the career ladder but have come in as part of a new policy of recruiting graduates. Such horizontal recruitment is likely to increase as the career ladder disappears; middle class men and women will be recruited for management positions.

Some women who went into banks about ten years ago have worked their way through to junior management positions. This was the period when the banks began to actively recruit women, and offer them the opportunity of a career. Here are some representative cases of the atypical few who have made it to career grades.

Accountant

Helen is a bright working class woman who joined the bank to please her mother, although she had wanted to go to university. She managed to avoid telling, a job which she regards as boring and unpleasant and moved quickly into examining. She has been in her current position for six years now and will need lending experience to get any further. Certainly she wants to move on; she claims that she's becoming 'part of the furniture'. Work makes her feel 'alive' and 'a real person'—she would hate to be at home all day. Helen was married briefly but now regards it as a bit of a mistake and sardonically views children as disastrous for women's lives. She discourages her own female staff from marriage—says that like herself they'll realise how bad it is and then have difficulties getting back into the workforce.

Accountant

Ruth is in her early 30s and is single. She has only just been appointed to this position although she had been relieving as an accountant for five years. She joined the bank twelve years ago via Centacom and regarded it as just another workplace. She still sees it as 'just a job'. 'Mind you most men of my age are managers—I'm even older than the manager here.' Ruth thinks the only reason she got promoted was because she is single. She knows good securities clerks with more experience who have not been promoted because they are married. Still, it is better to be in the bank—'outside I'd only be a typist'.

Secretary—staff club

Sandra is a working-class woman who started as a data processing machinist in 1972 and moved quite quickly through the all-female areas of EDP into a male area of EDP and now manages the staff club. Before the bank she worked for three and a half years in an insurance company doing clerical work and computer input. She left to go overseas and when she came back worked for six months as a cashier in Coles Supermarket. She has left the bank a couple of times to travel. After two years of machining she had become a supervisor; on returning from an overseas trip she went back into input/output, working shifts 'which wreck you'. She wanted to get out of production, and managed it. Her first appointment was in the chief manager's office, EDP. In her current position she has four women under her. The staff club handles staff discounts, theatre bookings, film processing, and travel. Although she hates the idea, she believes it is very important to have a male patron. 'You don't get anywhere unless there is someone up there pushing you when the opportunities come.'

These are all cases of working-class women who have experienced some upward mobility. But this is limited and, as Ruth in particular is aware, the status of management is questionable. Accountants are essentially supervisors, and as the role of branches is further downgraded, the status of most branch managers will also decline. With branch rationalisation their numbers will drop. There is very little opportunity for these women to move further up the ladder. Sandra is even more atypical than the accountants. Production areas in date processing are regarded as quite separate from the rest of the bank workforce, and apart from the rare exception, women never move out of them. It is worth noting again that none of these women is married. Other women we spoke to confirmed the view that management prefer single women.

What do women coming into banks now think about their job prospects? We sat in on an induction course for a group of about eight women. The one bloke who was meant to be there hadn't shown up. These young women were straight from school, and all of them lived in Sydney's western suburbs. They had been actively looking for jobs since about May of their HSC year. In answer to why did you choose banking they said that they did not choose. A couple of them had applied for apprenticeships with no success. They saw their job options as banking or the public service, with a preference for the latter. Their image of banking work: 'it's just clerical'. None see themselves as staying more than a couple of years. They want to use it as a way of getting into something more interesting. But if things went well they would consider staying to become accountants. They had been told about career possibilities in their initial interviews.

A continuing sexual division of labour

The opening up of the career structure to women, and formal equality of opportunity, have not led to a breaking down of the sexual division of labour. This division of labour has been maintained and extended. It has played a critical role in the gradual dismantling of the career structure.

Telling

Telling was once a prestigious job. Tellers had to be over 21, were usually 24–25, and had already worked in the bank for several years. It was the first step on the career ladder for young men. Now young people are moved quickly into telling with minimal knowledge of banking processes. The number of women on the counters has dramatically increased. However, women usually start on machines in the back office where most of them stay; whereas men move more quickly into telling and, with rare exceptions, never operate machines. It is a common complaint amongst the women that men are put on telling much earlier. A girl in one branch we visited had just been put on telling after two years whereas the boys went on after five months. Over and over again we have been told that girls pick things up more quickly, are more mature, and better tellers than boys. They know what they're doing because of the time spent in the back office. Because the blokes are hopeless they are quickly promoted off the telling line. 'Boys in banks look tatty, they don't even clean their shoes', said one female accountant. An administrator commented, 'Except with their mothers, they're hopeless. They don't know how to talk to customers, and they're immature, especially the Australian ones'.

The movement of women into telling is significant given the future prospects for this area of bank work. The major trend now is towards discouragement of personal transactions and services to the public. Automatic tellers will increasingly fulfil many of these functions—and for the remainder, customers are expected to queue up. Telling is now substantially keyboard work, as the details of transactions are punched directly into the computer. As happened previously with the ledger machines, women have moved into an area as it has become mechanised and the number of staff required are being drastically reduced.

The back office

In the back office junior clerical and machining work is almost exclusively performed by women. Ledger machinists have been replaced by 'input operators' and the work involves 'punching' or 'inputting' rather than 'posting'. Before the work is punched into the terminal it has to be proved or sorted and 'batching' is the term used for this. Operating machines is regarded as tedious work which the men are reluctant to do. It is generally believed that girls are better at detailed work, and that boys are more slapdash, and lack concentration on the machines. Women have greater manual dexterity and, given a routine, are less likely to depart from it. Sometimes it is acknowledged that women too get dissatisfied but this is resolved by moving them from one machine to another.

The other areas of back office work are examining and supervision. Examining, since computerisation, has become much more mundane, with minimal decision making involved. It is now done by both men and women. With the work process rationalised via machines, supervision has become less crucial and women hold a larger proportion of supervisory positions. Increasingly it is women that they are supervising—women on keyboard and machining work. We found that female supervisors frequently felt they were not getting their due. One, who had been with the bank for thirteen years, had been relieving classified officers for two years and has yet to receive a classified position herself. She felt that a man would have got this much earlier and that a woman had to work twice as hard to get recognition. (The assistant manager confirmed that he regarded her as his 'right hand', capable of any job in the bank.) Another senior woman put it more strongly. She felt there was almost a conspiracy against women. Not only were they not encouraged but those who did make it were denied further promotion. She cited cases of women who she felt had been 'kicked upstairs', pushed into deadend jobs.

The EDP centres

The work on machines and terminals done by batch clerks, savings bank clerks and input operators is probably best understood as part of an overall process, most of which takes place in EDP centres. The work now revolves around what happens in the centres rather than the branches.

The employment pattern in EDP centres throws some light on likely overall trends in banking, despite the fact that the numbers are relatively small. In a sense this is the whole point. Branches have the employment numbers; they need to be reduced. EDP has comparatively few and it does most of the work. It is treated as a relatively separate area, and recruitment has been on quite a different basis. People are employed for specific jobs and there is little mobility between different sections. The workforce is divided between the few highly paid jobs (systems analysts, programmers) and a larger number of routine jobs (machine operators, process workers). The latter area of work is described by management as 'the factory' and is staffed entirely by women. In chapter four we discuss in detail the sexual division of labour in data processing.

The main activity is clearance operations. As the computer runs 24 hours a day, this work is performed in shifts, the night shift consisting almost exclusively of married women, many of whom are migrants. These new jobs created by EDP have been hailed as offering women job opportunities. Yet if deskilling and degradation apply anywhere in the banks it is here. The women work under assembly-line conditions, with no possibility of advancement. Health problems are common, with regular complaints about colds, bronchitis, sinus, back and neck aches, eye strain, and an iritating itch from the machine area and stationery. We should perhaps be more cautious in using the term deskilled to describe this work. It does not take account of the skills required to cope with these job conditions and, furthermore, accuracy in punching is extremely important. Deskilled or not, these jobs are about to disappear. New proofing machines which are sixty times faster than the 'old' ones are being introduced. In this sense at least, the situation is similar to that in manufacturing.

Recruitment policy varies from bank to bank in the area of EDP. In most cases specialists, particularly analysts, were initially recruited from the bank. The reasons for this were the importance of loyalty to the bank and problems with breaking management resistance to computerisation. Analysts are in a strategic position as far as knowledge of the banking system goes. They, along with other specialists, have been paid the industry equivalent, rather than on the banks' scales, in order to attract and keep them. There is now a trend to recruit horizontally, that is, to employ experts from outside.

Programming is a very competitive area. Many people go into branches hoping to get into programming; bank computers are attractive because they are so big. We came across women in this situation who had experienced considerable difficulties: delays in starting training, being given clerical work during training, and at times sexual harassment. Sometimes they decide that branch work is preferable because women are treated better there. In summary, EDP has meant displacement of clerical positions in the branches. A new labour process has been created and a new job hierarchy set up, the most distinctive feature of which is the 'factory area' staffed by women.

Banking on the 'girls'

Bank work has become increasingly routinised and repetitive. The term deskilling could be applied in relation to changes in the content of 'mental' labour. Whereas in manufacturing it refers to the loss of knowledge and control associated with a combination of mental and manual skills, in white collar work such as banking it refers to a loss of knowledge of banking processes as a result of fragmentation. If it is used in this sense, then it is also middle class people, such as branch managers, who are experiencing a deskilling of their work. A woman who has been in the bank for forty years put it like this:

> I haven't been *opposed* to computers. . . . Some men and women accept that
> one no longer has complete knowledge of the job . . . it is no longer possible

to be an expert. There was once a time when there was very little that I didn't know.

There is now very little opportunity to move up the scale. The career structure has been gradually undermined and it is more than likely that management will abandon it completely in the near future. It is considered to be unwieldy and clearly its usefulness as a controlling ideology is wearing out. In its place a tiered structure is likely to be introduced. People will be recruited and paid for specific jobs from which there will be little opportunity to move. The Bank of New South Wales (Westpac) introduced a two-tier structure in December 1981: operational (School Certificate) and career (HSC). Sixty per cent of operations recruits are female. This bank is also recruiting graduates for future executive needs. Although some women will make it into the career strand, and female graduates are being recruited, this is linked to a relative shortage of male applicants. The bottom tier will be almost exclusively female. Women will again be formally locked into the lowest positions. The only exceptions will be tertiary educated, middle-class women.

The career structure was opened up to women at the very same time that it began to be dismantled. By increasing the proportions of women in the industry this process was obscured. Some career opportunities remained for the men, while women did the bulk of the low level work. Thus it could still appear that banking was a career industry offering upward mobility. Men could measure their career success against the work that women performed. As in the case of whitegoods, masculinity is potentially threatened; this time the middle-class masculinity associated with having a career. Again it is retained by virtue of the sexual division of labour. Loss of jobs at all levels could also be covered by natural wastage with women leaving at an early age. Given the current economic situation and the need for two incomes, they are less likely to leave now. With rationalisation and branch closures, sackings can be expected in the not too distant future.

As with whitegoods, this has not been a smooth process. Changes in the labour process took place under the guise of opening up job opportunities for women. Many women have become conscious of the fact that equal opportunities have been held out to them and yet men advance more quickly. They are angry about young inexperienced men moving ahead of them, and are aware that their capabilities are not being fully recognised or rewarded. Many have experienced hostility from men in the course of promotions. One of the ways in which women resolve this conflict is by participating in a redefinition of the gender of bank work. They will frequently say that they would not allow a son to go into banking. The women on the training course told us that it was seen as 'poofy'. Bank work is now women's work.

To return to the original sociological dilemma: most jobs in banks, as in other offices, can now be considered working class in that they are routine, repetitive, require and allow little knowledge of the overall process, and movement into management is restricted. Changes in the nature of bank work have been paralleled by a feminisation of the workforce. However, sociologists who attribute a division between white collar workers and blue collar workers to feminisation of white collar work are mistaken. In these accounts white collar work is defined as middle class because it is done by women, whose class position is defined either in terms of consciousness, or husband's class position. If the mental/manual distinction is continuing despite objective changes in the nature of mental labour it is because men in these white collar industries engage in 'mental' labour and make it into the middle class. The majority of women remain in 'manual' jobs. Whatever their consciousness, women occupy the newly created working class positions.

This is not to evade the question of industrial consciousness of white collar workers but rather to point out that any lack of militancy can not be attributed to some inherent conservatism of women. It is difficult and possibly dangerous to try and generalise about the trade union consciousness of bank workers. When asked 'would you attend union meetings', most of the women we spoke to demonstrated a lack of interest in the union. Yet it is not so much hostility as a belief that 'it doesn't do anything for us', or 'it is only concerned with trivia', or they displace responsibility by saying that 'bankies aren't interested', 'no-one goes on strike'. A trainee programmer who had been to union meetings didn't think the union was strong enough, but doesn't like militant unions. Some of the women who have now 'made it' were involved in the Women's Advisory Council, formed in the mid 60s to advise the CBOA on women's rights. Most of the women we spoke to are conscious of discrimination even if they don't see the union as the appropriate means for combatting it. The young women who described bank work as 'just clerical work', began by saying they wouldn't go to a union meeting, then said they would if they were going to lose their jobs or to gain an extra day's holiday or a pay rise.

Militant industrial consciousness is very seldom generated spontaneously. The bank unions, the CBOA and the Australian Bank Employees Union (ABEU), are militant as far as white collar unions go and have adopted a militant approach to technology and job loss. Yet they tend to accept the view that bankies are difficult to organise, and that women are particularly conservative. Our analysis of the position of women in the banks points to an alternative conclusion: women are less likely than men to accept the ideology of upward mobility, or the mystification of machines and ideology of progress that the banks have been using in their counter union compaigns.

3   Working at a discount
Retailing

Yes, women moved in during the war. But not into managerial jobs. The old blokes stayed in those. It was the young ones who went to the war and who the girls replaced. But it remained a man's domain after the war and the change was gradual. The 1950s were a key period. It's only in the last ten, twelve, fifteen years that there have been women in management. . . . They've taken away a little male kingdom. (Male department manager, age 55).

W OMEN moved into retailing, as in banking, in the 1950s: by 1974 they constituted 80 per cent of union membership. Unlike banking, retailing had always had a substantial minority of women working in clearly demarcated 'female' areas. Although white collar, retailing was in no sense middle class: shop assistants often earned less than labourers and most of the men, as well as the women, were outside of any career structure. At the same time retailing was portrayed as a 'respectable' occupation, a cut above factory work and indeed this ideology was used by the employers to justify low rates of pay and sweated labour. Retail workers struggled to attain a status as 'above' the working class. For the men this meant a battle to preserve 'their' areas against employers who would have preferred to bring in more women. Women earned only 54 per cent of the male rate until 1955, when it was increased to 75 per cent.

Retailing in its modern form emerged with the rise to prominence of the department stores in the 1880s. Before that, goods were sold either through markets and small shops or by larger specialist firms which bore a close resemblance to wholesalers. The distinction between wholesaling and retailing was not clear. While men monopolised the 'wholesaling' end, women were involved in small family businesses and frequently ran their own shops. Although much of the retail trade has remained in the hands of small shopkeepers, it is the development of wage labour in retailing that we shall be primarily concerned with in this chapter.

Women moved into shopwork as a clearly preferred alternative to domestic service. They were often the daughters of tradesmen who did not want them to go into the factories. Retailing seemed to provide some independence and a degree of status. Ironically, the occupation it most resembled probably *was* domestic service. Shoppers could expect an extraordinary degree of servility and obsequiousness from shop assistants who were, quite literally, their servants. Shop assistants may have been proud to work for these large stores, just as servants identified with the values of the households for whom they worked, but their status as *servants* was nonetheless clear to their employers and to those who patronised the shops (Pratt, 1978; Dunstan, 1979; Maccul- loch, 1980). Until the first award came into effect, in 1907 in NSW, they could be made to work for nothing for the first six months, and then receive as little as 2/6d. per week. Employers liked female assistants to be 'respectable', that is, living at home. If they were not married by the time they were 23, when the full adult rate was paid, they suffered a double indignity: they were sneered at for not finding husbands while, at the same time, they had to keep their age down or they were likely to be sacked.

Employers were always keen to take on more women: the first half of this century saw a running battle between employers wanting to extend the number of departments in which women could work and male- dominated unions trying to preserve their male members' wages and working conditions by restricting them. This was exacerbated by the development of chain or variety stores (Coles and Woolworths) in the 1920s. These stores emphasised cheapness ('Nothing over 2/6d') and largely took the service element out of selling. They tried to avoid paying the award by reclassifying their workers as packers and wrappers. The union took them to court to establish that all such workers were covered by the shop assistants' award. It was also concerned about the employment implications but was less successful in the campaign to organise a public boycott of the self-service stores (*The Shop Assistant*, January 1934).

The sexual division of labour in retailing was difficult to rationalise in terms of the actual physical tasks. As elsewhere, men were allocated the 'heavy' areas like furniture, hardware and carpets. But beyond this, much rested on what it was considered 'seemly' for men and women to sell and the likely gender of the customer. In addition, there were areas where either sex was considered appropriate. It was here that the employers attempted to increase the proportion of women, who they could employ so much more cheaply. By 1938 the NSW Industrial Court had to make a clear ruling on these three areas. This was important because it defined the broad contours of retail work until the 1972 equal pay case.

The 1938 Award stipulated that in 'unisex' areas at least fifty per cent men had to be employed. It did not forbid the employment of women in male areas as long as they were paid the male rate. The union hailed this as a move towards 'equal pay' while at the same time it acknowledged that its main purpose was to protect male jobs: 'It will give protection to the trade against a class of store that employs all female labour, some of which are notorious for the low wages that their shops are run on' (*The Shop Assistant*, July 1938). It was assumed that, without a pay differential, employers would automatically prefer a man.

The definition of men's and women's departments shows up the full extent to which work was organised around gender. It also points to the ways in which gender is itself constructed at work.

Men's departments

1 Groceries (a time-honoured category of men's work, going back to its associations with wholesaling and the notion of the grocer as the skilled all-rounder; sale of biscuits, cakes and confectionery were specifically excluded)
2 Men's clothing
3 Youth's clothing
4 Hardware (excluding kitchen or household items, crockery and glassware)
5 Furniture (excluding baby furniture)
6 Carpets and linoleum
7 Manchester, other than fancy linen, napery and towels
8 Mercery
9 Men's hats
10 Youths' hats
11 Men's footwear
12 Youths' footwear
13 Sports goods
14 Saddlery and trade grindery
15 Wireless sets and equipment
16 Motor vehicles and accessories
17 Bicycles and accessories

Women's departments

1–7 Women's and girls': outer garments, under garments, hosiery, gloves, neckwear, handkerchieves, footwear
8 Boys' and girls' footwear
9 Corsetry
10 Furs
11 Millinery
12 Handbags
13 Baby wear
14 Baby furniture
15 Toilet requisites
16 Perfumery
17 Knitting wools
18 Haberdashery, including ribbons and laces
19 Artificial flowers

20   Fancy or art jewellery
21   Toys
22   Paper patterns
23   Fancy needlework
24   Sunshades and umbrellas
25   Small ecclesiastical and devotional articles
26   Flowers, foliage, decorative fruits and berries, plants and seedlings
27   Cakes and pastry
(*The Shop Assistant*, July 1938)

This list points to the ways in which commodities were being used in the *construction* of sexual identity. They were not just commodities with a use value but carried strong messages about masculinity and femininity.

It was not until during and after World War II that women came to be spread more widely through retailing and only comparatively recently that they have moved into junior management. During the war there were many disputes as women went before the Women's Employment Board to claim the male rate for the work they were doing. They did not always succeed. For example, although men had worked in silk and dress goods departments, the Industrial Commission varied the award to allow the employers to pay female rates (*The Shop Assistant*, January 1943). The union was adamant that:

> Males must not be displaced. If it is found that there is some difficulty in replacements surely the men who have grown too old at forty might be permitted to come back into the trade . . . it would be some guarantee to those who leave their employment for military purposes that the jobs are in the safe keeping of senior men (*The Shop Assistant*, January 1940).

The men did, in fact, return to their jobs after the war and changes came only slowly. For example, in 1948 the Retail Traders Association moved to have electrical goods deleted from the equal pay provisions of the award (*The Shop Assistant*, July-September 1948). The clearcut sexual division of labour continued and some aspects of it are still with us in the 1980s. Ladies underwear and furniture are still clearly sex segregated.

In the 1950s women were able to move into a wider range of clerical and sales areas without threatening men's jobs. There was a labour shortage and fewer men were attracted into mainstream retailing. They could make more money elsewhere. The pay and status of retailing declined compared with other parts of the tertiary sector. These changes coincided with the continuous reorganisation of the labour process, with the growing proportion of unskilled jobs in the industry and with the application of new technologies.

Self-service in the suburbs

The consumption boom meant, to state the obvious, that there were a lot more things for people to buy: clothing and processed foods, whitegoods and electrical appliances. Increasingly, goods arrived from the warehouse prepackaged and ready for immediate sale. 'Finished' items had once been the luxury consumption of the middle class. Clothes were largely made at home or by dressmakers/tailors. Foods were less processed which meant larger bulk sales of items like flour and sugar. The shop assistant's job involved not only selling but measuring, cutting, lifting, stacking, fitting and packaging. That is, turning goods into saleable form. Thus, for example, many of the women came in with a background in dressmaking or millinery: skills that were to be phased out.

Until the late 1950s, shopping habits were characterised by frequent trips, by public transport or on foot, to purchase food and groceries, and occasional trips to the city for the larger items. As Australians acquired their first motor cars and moved further out into the suburbs, retailing patterns changed. In Sydney the shift from trams and ferries to buses and trains had already caused big upheavals, in the interwar years. This was as nothing compared with the rise of the motor car, which accentuated the trend to suburban shopping.

In the early 1960s the supermarket appeared almost overnight. In Melbourne, by 1961–62 self-service establishments had 71 per cent of the grocery trade with only 16 per cent of the outlets (Johnston and Rimmer, 1969: 41). The essence of the supermarket is self-service, with 'selling' staff substantially replaced by cashiers and those pricing the goods and refilling the shelves. This changes dramatically the nature of the work and the relationship between shop assistant and customer.

The shift to the suburbs made jobs more accessible to married women with children. The supermarket concept made nonsense of the old division between men's and women's areas of employment. Large numbers of women were employed in the supermarkets as cashiers. Male grocers and other small shopkeepers were simultaneously displaced, leaving rows of dead empty shops in what had once been busy neighbourhood shopping centres. The result was a massive feminisation of retailing coinciding with a growing proportion of wage labour.

The department stores were also forced to seek suburban locations and to apply self-service techniques. The first regional shopping centre was opened at Chermside, near Brisbane in 1958. Within two years similar centres had followed at Top Ryde in Sydney and Chadstone in Melbourne. In the 1960s a further twenty regional and community shopping centres and ten major stores were opened in Sydney suburbs. Similar developments took place in all the major cities and in the big country centres.

By the 1970s the retailers were in trouble. Many of the best known names had already gone out of business and the very concept of the department store was under challenge. The recession, combined with the slackening of population growth, meant that sales growth slowed down and gross margins were cut. The big firms came under heavy pressure from discount houses and the techniques were quickly applied first to supermarkets and then to department stores themselves.

Discounting involves high volume, fast turnover and lower profit margins. It has forced the retailers to streamline their buying procedures and to take advantage of economies of scale. This in turn has brought about further concentration in the industry.

Structural change

At one end of the retail trade is G.J. Coles and Company, the largest private employer in Australia after BHP. At the other is the corner grocery store, unable to compete except by opening for very long hours, and the boutique catering more to the quality end of the market. Because of this diversity the retail sector is less concentrated than, say, the manufacturing sector. Nevertheless the industry is now dominated by what have come to be known as the 'Big Six': Coles, Woolworths, Myer, Grace Bros., David Jones and Waltons. Coles and Myer are based in Melbourne, the other four in Sydney although controlling interests in David Jones and Waltons are now outside NSW. Woolworths and Coles achieved their position through variety stores in the interwar period, and later, supermarkets and discount stores. Together they now account for almost forty per cent of the food market. Coles, in partnership with the US firm, SS Kresge, developed the single-floor freestanding K-Mart discount store with a food supermarket alongside. This has become the model for all other firms.

Woolworths moved into supermarkets following its takeover of McIlwraiths, the old-style grocery chain, in the 1950s. In the 1960s it added Flemings (NSW), Nancarrow in Victoria, BCC in Queensland and Food Fair in WA. Waltons rose to power by taking over a series of old department stores in the sixties: Marcus Clarks, Anthony Horderns, Mark Foys and McDowells. This was described as an 'attack by a nouveau riche from the Western Suburbs on Sydney's retail establishment' (*Australian Financial Review*, 10 December 1971). The remaining three are old established department stores. David Jones was taken over by The Adelaide Steamship Company in July 1980. Since then it too has had to lose its staid image and apply discounting techniques.

The industry is currently undergoing a further restructuring of ownership. The big discount house, Norman Ross, has now been taken over by Waltons Bond after a court battle with Grace Bros. The future

WHAT'S

THE

DIFFERENCE?

Dusting the escalators, department store

GENDER & WORK

PRODUCING

Honorary: civilian clothes
Resident: white coat

Resident: long white coat
Medical student: short
white coat

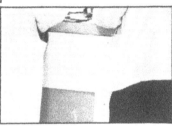

Resident: white coat over civilian clothes
Charge sister: blue uniform

Registered nurse: striped
uniform

1st year student nurse:
one stripe

DIFFERENCE

White shoes: student nurse
Black shoes: registered nurse

Student nurse in theatre:
Masculine? Feminine?

Male student nurse:
Pale blue-striped uniform

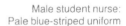

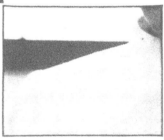

Wardsman: brown uniform

It is essential to take account of the ways in which gender relations and class relations shape each other. This is as much the case in relation to work as in other spheres of social existence.

domestic/labour

Bank of New South Wales
Sydney 4th. July, 1907.

Dear Mr. Miller,

As some proof of the superiority
of women-typists over the typist-masculine,
I submit for your and the General Manager's
inspection, three specimens of duplicating
work from our Department, done by Miss
Miller. I am perfectly sure you would
never get any boy or man to take so much
trouble or do the work so neatly and ex-
peditiously. And if men were ever to
adopt typewriting as a profession, I am
afraid in years to come you could never
expect competent General Managers, Inspec-
tors, Chief Accountants, &c. &c., - for my
opinion of typewriting is that it is a dis-
tinctly stultifying, somewhat intellect
destroying occupation and calculated to
produce want of enterprise.

Yours truly,

Typewriting Department.

AND NOW, ON KEYBOARDS..

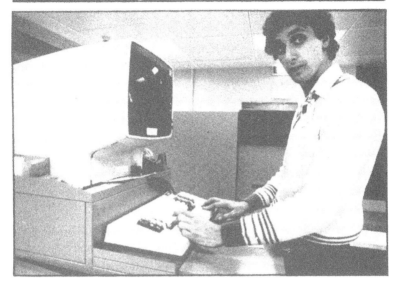

EDP Centre: banking

Phototypesetter: printing

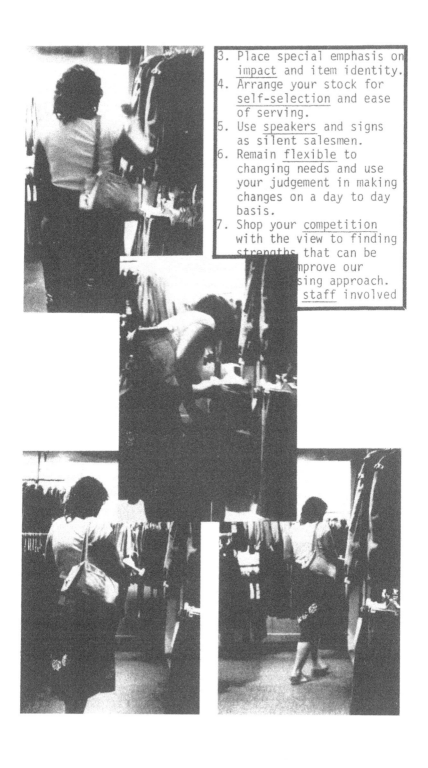

3. Place special emphasis on impact and item identity.
4. Arrange your stock for self-selection and ease of serving.
5. Use speakers and signs as silent salesmen.
6. Remain flexible to changing needs and use your judgement in making changes on a day to day basis.
7. Shop your competition with the view to finding strengths that can be
   mprove our
   sing approach.
   staff involved

SELF-SELECTION

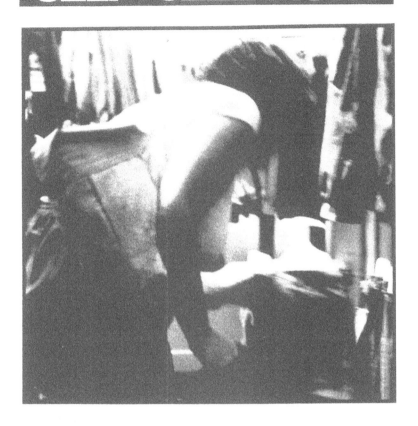

WORKING

IN YOUR

LUNCH-HOUR

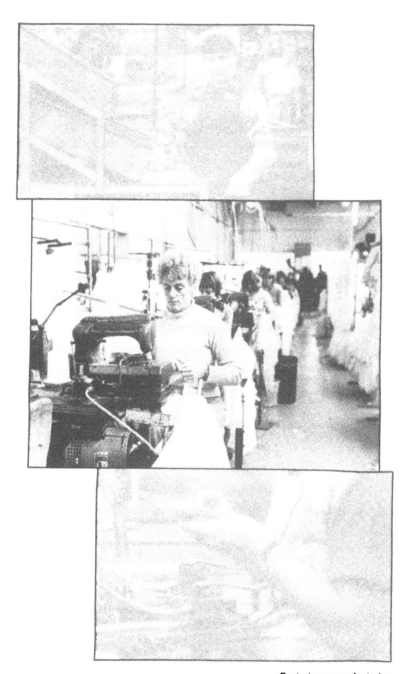

Factories: manufacturing

Factories: white-collar

Money market, banking

Junior filing clerk (male), banking

Textiles mill, cotton spinning

of Grace Bros. remains in doubt, following takeover bids from both Waltons and Woolworths.

The other major development has been the arrival of the American fast food chains. By 1980 there were 195 Kentucky Fried Chicken outlets, 98 Pizza Huts and 116 McDonalds.

Automation

Computerisation commenced in the middle to late 1960s, greatly facilitated by the concentration we have described. At first it involved single functions, most obviously the payroll system, which mainly affected clerical staff. More recently it has been applied to electronic cash registers and point-of-sale terminals. Self-service was combined with centralised cash-and-wrap facilities operated by fulltime cashiers who do not leave the terminals.

It was not a foregone conclusion that the supermarket checkout operators would be women. After the 1972 equal pay decision Woolworths began to train boys but as the work became more automated it reverted to females. They still do claim to train boys, and have used them in setting up new stores, but within a few months the boys miraculously disappear. It is clearly seen as 'women's' work 'like using a typewriter' and boys are not enthusiastic about taking it on.

The first phase of computerisation was in the area of data collection, with NCR cash registers being connected to a head office computer. Instead of relying on weekly sales, instant and detailed sales information was now available. The checkout operator punches in not only the price but a code number for the category of each item. Decisions about purchases, advertising and promotions are now taken at head office. In addition to compiling accounts records, the microprocessor based registers can control stock levels, re-order, read merchandise labels and credit cards. They are compatible with automatic tellers such as Westpac's Handybank system. This means that the 'cashless society' may soon be at hand, as we will be able to instantly debit our accounts with some more advanced form of bankcard. According to recent experiments such transactions can be conducted in less than a third of the time of a conventional one (*Bankers Magazine*, February 1981).

The brave new world of Universal Product Code (UPC) is almost upon us. Electronic scanning systems, using this code, are likely to be introduced shortly. The zebra-striped symbol on a label or packet, which is now used by more than 700 Australian manufacturers, (*The Advertiser*, 2 June 1982), can be read by an instore mini-computer. It interprets the symbol, looks up the price and item description, transmits this to the cash register, where it is displayed to the customer and printed on a detailed receipt tape. It is claimed that this is thirty per cent faster than the regular keying-in of prices; there are no errors; there is a permanent record of purchases and an accurate record of what has been sold. It is also claimed to be quieter and less fatiguing than having to hunt around for a smudged price to ring up (*Australian*, 9 March 1979). As we shall see, it has rather more devastating implications for the workforce. There is also a lot of customer resistance to not being able to check the price directly on the goods. The first Australian testing has been taking place in Hobart, Bendigo, and Coonabarabran (*Australian Financial Review*, 30 June 1980), at Sims in Melbourne and Foodland at Clare in South Australia (*The Advertiser*, 2 June 1982). Meanwhile Woolworths has a half-way version which it is testing at Arncliffe and at the Macquarie Centre in Sydney, where a code number rather than a price is punched into the terminal.

The other big changes are in warehousing. This has traditionally been a male area which is justified in terms of the scale of the operations, handling bulk items. Computers can now control the level of stock and direct collection from the store. It has already happened with reserve stock and will soon be applied to the 'picking face'. That is, the computer will inform the forklift driver what goods are to be assembled and where they are located. It is only a matter of time before the driver too becomes redundant. Because it facilitates the management of stocks, the attendant costs of insurance, interest and rent of space are reduced; fewer clerical workers, as well as storemen, are needed. As automation proceeds we may expect to see a higher proportion of women in the warehouses. Certainly they are present at David Jones and Grace Bros, though at Woolworths they are restricted to the general merchandise area. Although the workforce in warehouses is being reduced, it is potentially industrially powerful. As the amount of stock in hand at any time is reduced with this form of warehousing, industrial action will have a more decisive effect on the firm.

Gender and the labour process

Changes in the organisation of work and in the composition of the workforce have been predicated on gender division and hierarchy. Job fragmentation is most clearly seen in the case of the supermarkets. Here selling functions are minimal and the employees are classified as cashier, shelf filler, bagger or supervisor. As we have seen, the cashiers are predominantly women, despite some half-hearted attempts to train men by companies anxious to be seen to be non-discriminatory. They are expected to wear a uniform, are often forbidden to wear slacks and are not allowed to wear anything over their uniforms even when it's cold. The 'Checkout Chicks' (a particularly offensive management term) are made to feel 'pretty stupid'—'If people want to think that,

that's their problem—I can't saying anything because it *is* a pretty stupid job'. The cashier is virtually indistinguishable from a factory operative. She constantly moves products along a mini-conveyor belt and quickly records the prices. As scanning comes in she will simply pass the item over the scanner and the register will transmit the operation to a computer. This task too could be allocated to the customer, though it is said that the checkout operators will remain: 'women customers need the company'. Meanwhile the 'production' of each register can be monitored from a single central station and laggards noted for future action. Since no knowledge of prices is required, the production speed can be pegged at the highest level within a few hours of beginning the job.

There is much debate about the extent of deskilling in this job. The Shop, Distributive and Allied Employees Association (SDA) claim that a 'reskilling' process has taken place. They say that whereas anyone could operate a manual cash register it now takes months to master all the codes and a lot of people drop out because they can't cope with it. The checkout operators we spoke to claimed that the job could be picked up in as little as a week but spoke of a number of difficulties associated with their work. One is the need for concentration over long periods of time. Staff are under constant surveillance. In one store we visited the manager observed staff through a one-way window and appeared frequently to tell people what they were doing wrong. There is considerable pressure as a result of understaffing. If customers have to wait in a long queue they tend to take it out on the checkout 'girl'. Staff are threatened with the sack if they are too slow or if their tills do not balance.

Most of the stacking is now done by night fillers, who replenish and price new stock which arrives on pallets from a warehouse laid out in the same manner as the supermarket. There have been changes in the organisation of selling space over the last ten years. Once each store was given general instructions: 'allow twenty feet for the soups!'. Now they are shown exactly what lines to put where. Laying out the shelves is done by specialists working off planograms. The night fillers commence work after normal trading hours at six pm and are not meant to work past midnight. However, they frequently work till two am and receive only the ordinary wages for working overtime. All the goods must be rotated according to how old they are. In one company the pressure has been increased by the introduction of a time sheet based on a time and motion study. This fosters competition between workers and forces them to speed up.

The night fillers were initially men, chosen because of the heavy work involved. Management were reluctant to employ women because of the 'hanky panky' they imagined would go on in the dark! But the majority (80–90 per cent) are now women, mostly older married women. We were told that this change resulted from changes in the taxation system. Once everybody had to fill out rebate forms, people started to work under assumed names. The companies could not condone this and there was pressure to put people off. 'Consequently the men dropped off and their wives went out to do it instead'. It just so happened that this has coincided with further changes. Nightfilling was introduced by Safeways, following the American example, to try and attract people away from the busier days. Obviously it is more pleasant shopping if you're not falling over people doing stacking all around you. But Thursday night shopping has meant that the supermarkets are relatively empty in the early part of the week. Consequently there has been a move back to day filling, which is also cheaper since night rates do not have to be paid. It can be argued that this move has been made a lot easier by the presence of a more flexible female workforce.

Amongst the other supermarket jobs, bagging and parcel pickup tends to be done by young boys. Again, they have relative mobility compared with the checkout people. Supervision of checkout women is done by women. Men don't want it because they see it as women's work and there would, anyway, be a lot of resistance from the women.

In the department stores the variety of work done by shop assistants has been greatly reduced. Categories like floorwalkers have long disappeared. Even in the 'big ticket items' of electrical goods and furniture, there is less emphasis on service and product knowledge. In traditional service areas like clothing and footwear, customers receive little assistance. The only new staff carry out a policing function checking customers in and out of the change rooms to make sure that they don't steal anything. Even if staff accumulate experience there is little opportunity for them to 'assist' customers. Personalised selling has been replaced by advertising, which is done by specialists.

Retailing employs many clerical workers. Their work too has changed, as has the ratio of clerical to sales staff. Charles Lloyd Jones estimated that thirty years ago his company had 1.5/1.6 employees behind the scenes for every shop floor assistant. Now there are 1.5 or more sales assistants for every administrative worker (*National Times*, 3 March 1979). This has been achieved partly by the ending of 'luxuries' like mail order departments, no longer required as the stores opened branches in the country. But more significantly, there has been a streamlining of credit, merchandising, personnel, buying and ware-housing functions.

Office work is women's work and here, as elsewhere, the majority of clerical workers have been women. In the collection areas they quite deliberately employ 'mature women', many of them divorced or separated and in similar positions to the women at the other end of the phone in terms of coping with financial hardship. These women are encouraged to see their role in terms of 'marriage counselling'. Men retain most of the managerial, though not the supervisory positions. There have recently been moves to bring a few men into clerical work to 'smarten up the girls'. Thus management is at times prepared to reverse gender conventions about the division of labour in order to improve its control.

Fast foods: the shape of things to come?

The fast food firms have broken up the labour process to an extent we would not have thought possible a few years ago. They have relied heavily, first on women, and then on teenage casual workers of both sexes. Employees are expected to perform in clockwork fashion. At McDonalds they are in a sense programmed, complete with specifically-worded interchanges for the brief customer encounters. The nature of the work may best be illustrated by reference to one of the checksheets provided, in this case to those engaged in preparing and assembling a 'burger'.

Quarter pound buns
When a call for ten quarters is received by the grillman
1 Place bun crowns on bun tray cut side up.
2 Place bun heels on spatula cut side down.
3 When the turn buzzer on the quarter pound timer sounds and the grillman says '*turning quarters*':
   a   Place the crowns on the bun tray into the bottom section of the quarter pound toaster and pull the handle down.
   b   The heels on the spatula are placed on top of the bunboard.
4 After *55 seconds* buzzer will sound, pull back the handle and remove the crowns and place on the preparation table to be dressed.
5 Then the bunman places the heels underneath the bunboard and removes the spatula. The spatula is placed on top of the bunboard.
6 As the grillman removes the meat he calls '*Quarter heels please*'. The bunman removes the heels from the toaster and places them on top of the dressed crowns and meat.

Dressing quarter pounders
1 Separate the buns
2 Dress the buns:

quarter pound	quarter pound—cheese
1 shot mustard	1 shot mustard
1 shot ketchup (use /H lever)	1 shot ketchup (use /H lever)
16 to 22 cubes of onion	16 to 22 cubes of onion
2 pickles (3 if under 1″)	2 pickles (3 if under 1″)
	2 slices of cheese (one for style).

3 To determine the number of quarter pounders with cheese the dress person says to the production caller—'cheese on ten quarters please'.
4 After receiving and acknowledging the call the first slice of cheese is placed on the appropriate number of crowns and the second slice is placed on the bun tray.

As in the supermarkets, looks and personality are important for the female seeking casual employment. Girls are mostly stationed 'out the front', that is, selling, while the boys are mostly 'out the back' in the food area. The companies deny that this is a conscious policy but at the same time present a stereotype of female and male roles:

> During a busy period, the young guys like the challenge of running the grill. It's very hot and it needs a lot of coordination. The challenge doesn't appeal so much to the young girls. The young girls tend to be more pleasant and more articulate and are therefore suited to the selling area.

The labour process of management

In the 1970s, when it was decided that management in retailing was 'top heavy', the efficiency experts were called in. As a result the 'fat' has been cut from all levels of management, personnel and staff training as well as from the clerical and sales areas. At times this has meant that juniors are doing work that was once done by more senior staff:

> There used to be a personnel manager, personnel officer and three fulltime clerks. Then it was reduced to four when one of the clerks went. Then the personnel officer went and was not replaced—and another clerk left. Finally they decided, no more personnel managers! The manager was replaced by a personnel officer. And when she left I took over and wasn't even upgraded. (Female personnel clerk)

Middle management has been cut back severely, with categories like 'merchandise manager' or 'controller' disappearing entirely in some firms:

> It's now very difficult to get from DM to store manager. All the steps in between have been removed. This took place before cuts in shop floor staff. (Female section head)

Staff are working under a lot more pressure:

> The hierarchy is always demanding more and it's not enough. I work from eight till six, nine-thirty or later on Thursdays and eat lunch on the phone. (Female assistant store manager)

> You get commission if you can get the budget—but budgets are a little bit unrealistic. (Female section head)

These comments come from women. They have moved rapidly into junior 'management' positions over the last ten years or so and this is related to changes in the labour process of management. We need to ask, what counts as 'management', and how do we distinguish managerial workers from the rest?

'Management' officially begins at the level of Department Manager.

This is the point at which people are discouraged from staying in the union—many believe that they have to actually leave. And yet they earn a mere $250 a year more:

> They cop it because they're on the ladder . . . but what if the ladder doesn't really exist . . . they're worried. (Union organiser)

The work is mostly about supervising and motivating the staff and taking responsibility for the level of sales. In talking to women department managers we were struck by the overlap with the mothering role, with the willingness to shoulder the burden of the smooth running of the department, to anticipate what has to be done and get stuck in and do it:

> Everyone needs to spend time on the floor, even the managing director. A bloke in my position would sit in the office and turn it into a cushy job. I rush about. Ladies work much harder than men.

> A man will *tell* you to do things. A lady boss is a little more understanding and you know more about the work that's involved.

> Men in furniture wouldn't even lift a coffee table. They'd get the cleaners to lift anything. You should see what we lift here [manchester]. When I was in furniture I moved it. I even move fixtures. Women get things done, they have more brains about it. Men are fussy about their status.... Mind you I'm not a man-hater.

As with mothers, their power operates only over a limited domain. They rarely have much to do with buying or advertising and their job focusses on organising other staff and for much of the time working side by side with them.

Yet the status of 'management' operates as a powerful incentive. It gives them a place in the world, 'above' the ordinary workers. This gives people a feeling of upward mobility, a sense that they have 'made it' out of the working class. Top management exploits this as an alternative to *paying* them for the sheer quantity of work they do. In this respect it operates very similarly to the ideology of 'respectability' earlier in the century. This is very clear in the case of the small shops. To say that you are the 'manager of a boutique' sounds impressive—but it may simply mean that you are paid award wages and have one person to help you. If you are lucky you will get a small commission.

Much the same applies to buying. It is supposedly the 'glamour' side of retailing. Yet even if they do control a large budget and score trips to Hong Kong and Taiwan they operate under severe constraints and according to a tightly organised schedule. Women have moved into this area. In some firms they are restricted to children's clothing and items that are regarded as requiring a woman's eye for colour combinations; in others they are spread more widely. But few have made it to the senior levels.

Even at the junior level women still do not compete on equal terms with men:

> My DM is male. He started on the same training course and got the same marks as I did. Given that I've 'wasted' four years here I might as well stick it out a bit longer. (Section Head)

> The men who come into retailing know they're going to become managers. They don't go around saying, I'm better than you, but they really think they are. (Section Head)

When women do get into management they are likely to be paid considerably less than their male counterparts. It is difficult to find out how much people are paid because it is a closely guarded secret. Salaries and promotions are individually negotiated in retailing: this is part of the ethos. And it works against women. As we have seen in banking, they are much more likely to get 'equal' treatment in a bureaucratic structure where salary scales are clearly laid out.

It is often suggested that women won't push themselves, or that they are afraid to take responsibility. Yet, as the following comment makes clear, this is to take things right out of context. Women are operating in a situation where they feel they have no rightful authority—if they are afraid to take responsibility there is a good reason for it:

> You'll ask them to take on some supervisory function and two responses are very likely. Either they'll say 'sure' and then do nothing about it; or they'll say, no, that's not for me. They don't like having power over the other women, can't handle it. They worry about things like how they'll be able to go on having morning tea together—they don't seem to be able to exercise power over each other and stay friendly. Whereas men can usually do this easily. There may be hard words but it won't spoil the relationship. Women seem to think they oughtn't have authority over each other. And thirdly, few women feel they should compete with men—even where they are in roughly the same position they'll defer to the man, you see it over and over again. And maybe if there's a job he's not interested in doing he'll shrug and say, here, you do it. And they will. (Female administrator, retailing computer centre)

Just because women have moved into retailing it would be a mistake to think they are there on equal terms. We found a stronger resistance to women at the top than we did even in banking. Men have taken steps to ensure that the 'real' managerial positions remain theirs. While no longer 'paternalistic', retailing remains strongly *patriarchal*—the names of the big companies, for instance are all *male* names. The family traditions of these firms are about the Sons taking over from the Fathers. While women are acceptable in personnel, in computing areas and in the departments, they remain a minority in buying. There are no women store managers (except for tiny backwaters) and no expectations that there will be any in the immediate future. They have to content themselves with being the 'power behind the throne':

> My immediate group manager thinks I should push on to become a store
> manager, but I don't know that it matters. I get my way even if he thinks the
> ideas are his. Men are like children in some ways. (Assistant store manager)

This woman has rationalised the power relation by thinking that she
controls him as a child. Men can behave like children while still
exercising power and control; they have fragile egos but continue to
dominate, and treat the world as their rightful inheritance.

The status of retailing—up or down?

The simple answer is that it has remained much the same as it always
was. The majority of people in retailing are struggling to preserve a
status slightly above manual workers. It is an occupation that seems to
hold out the possibility of some upward mobility for working class
people but the shifting proportion of men and women has changed the
situation in ways that are worth exploring. Despite what we have said
about patriarchy, the status of men in retailing has dropped since the
war and that of women has improved. This does not mean that
patriarchy is about to be toppled, but it does mean that women are
better placed to fight it than they used to be: they are in no sense passive
victims.

With the expansion of mass consumption in the 1950s, retailing
attained a certain glamour, perhaps because of its association with the
growing advertising industry. Thus it was an attractive proposition for
some men. It was seen as less stuffy than banking or the public service.
'People who mucked up in school tended to go into it.' Men who had
missed out on a government job or failed first year university knew that
in retailing they could still reach managerial level and eventually earn a
reasonable income. Arthur, now aged 55, joined Winns forty years ago.
He says: 'There was a lot more kudos in retailing then and it was quite
competitive to get in'. Frank, slightly younger, started as a Hordern's
cadet in 1951. 'There were twelve trainees, all male. I decided I liked
retailing better than farming as my father had done—living like a
peasant. My uncle had some secondhand shops and I used to help him
after school'. These men are happy with their careers but would not
want to see their sons in retailing and would not go into it themselves if
they were starting now. They mentioned deskilling, the limited
opportunities for promotion and the declining status of lower managerial positions. And they cited friends who had made a lot more money
buying grog shops or selling real estate. Because men were allowed
higher expectations they had, in a sense, further to drop. And many
dropped out altogether, effectively making way for the women:

Not a lot of men want to work in retailing—at least in selling. It's not
financially rewarding for a breadwinner unless he's earning a commission.
You could get as much as a labourer. (Male personnel manager)

For women the situation is more complex. *Their* jobs *never* carried
much status. They have gained access to a wider ranger of jobs as the
feminisation of the area proceeded. Formally they have equal pay and
some have made it a short way up the 'ladder'. A high proportion are
married and bring the 'status' of marriage to work in a way that men
cannot. Class is not defined purely by occupation or 'relation to the
means of production'; and women are at times able to turn their status
as wives and mothers to advantage. Take the case of Mrs B. She is now
fifty, has been married 31 years and has four adult children. Her
husband was a successful builder until he had a stroke and they have a
comfortable home plus swimming pool in Sydney's western suburbs.
She was out of the workforce for nearly twenty years before returning to
work as a casual cash-and-wrap 'girl'. She rapidly pushed her way up to
become assistant store manager. Hers is one of the more spectacular
success stories. How did she do it? She presents the stereotype of the
retailing person: hair up high, rings on the fingers, heavily made up and
dressed in a smart casual suit. She was very 'laid back', with a common,
casual touch, lots of rough talk and an obvious sexual confidence. This
confidence comes out of a successful marriage 'partnership', material
prosperity and a strong sense of her place in the world. All of this was
brought to bear on her work environment, enabling her to overcome
the obstacles that most women experience.

Mrs B is an exceptional case. But the following comments from
working class women in more precarious situations also suggest a
certain self-confidence:

I got in seventeen years ago by accident. I was offered a 'man's job' by a
friend of the family doing home service for Buckingham's. My kids were
three and five at the time and I had to support them. Eventually I got into
buying exclusive kids' wear. At about this time I decided finally to kick my
husband out.

Our fourth child, a girl, had to have open-heart surgery and it cost a packet.
One day I was walking past Hordern's mid-city and I saw an advertisement
for casuals. I thought, here's a go. So up the stairs I went and filled out an
application form.... My husband didn't like it but I assured him it was only
till Christmas. Christmas came and went and I'm still here [ten years later].

I used to run my own deli in the mountains. Then I had an accident and my
staff bought me out. My mother had worked for Walton's as a casual and I
started there too, as a casual on the credit counter.

My husband's a drunk and I've got three kids to support. I've been here
twelve years now.... Before my marriage I worked in Anthony Hordern's
mail order section so I knew a bit about accounts.

These cases are interesting for what they show about power relations in the family—something we return to in the chapter on housework. The confidence of these women is connected with authority in the domestic sphere. Either they are in the workforce because of their husbands' lack of success at work and consequent loss of authority at home, or their going to work has given them a sense of strength in relation to their husbands. Similar complexities in the power relations within the family have been found by the authors of *Making the Difference*, an important recent study of class and gender relations in schools and families (Connell, Ashenden, Kessler, Dowsett, 1981).

Retailing is known as a 'threshold industry'. It is often the first job people take on and it is attractive to women coming back to the workforce after having children. These women know what retailing is about—they are familiar with it as shoppers. They show a lot of pride and courage in coping with what are often very difficult personal situations, and are not going to be easily pushed around. Even in adversity they bring a 'substance' with them to the workplace. Unfortunately, as in banking, this has often served to obscure the actual nature of the work and the processes of fragmentation and casualisation that are taking place.

Casualisation and gender

The most striking recent development in retailing has been the growing proportion of casual staff. Because wholesaling and retailing are conflated in the official statistics it is difficult to get a precise picture. While the part-time workforce has more than doubled in the past decade, the full-time workforce has been pruned considerably. Of the 90,500 part-time jobs created between August 1973 and August 1980, 82 per cent were taken by women (ABS, the Labour Force, 1981). Retailing has thus seen a massive switch from a full-time to a casual and part-time workforce. Why?

Partly it is linked to rationalisation, structural and technological change. With self-service there is no longer any need for the customer to be served in each separate department. The decline of selling functions means there is less demand for product knowledge or specific selling skills. In considering the 'feminisation' of retailing we should not forget how much of the work has been taken over by (unpaid) women shoppers—it is not accidental that housewives spend a lot more time shopping than they did in the past. Queensland's Jack the Slasher, before he was taken over by Safeways, advertised:

Ladies, if you don't need servants at home, you don't need them in this warehouse. You price your own goods, pack your own goods at the checkout.

(Bring your own bags—we're fresh out.) Push your goods to your car and save money. (*Bulletin*, 10 February 1980)

This, of course, did not mean an easier time for shop assistants, merely a reduction of the ratio of staff to sales and more concentrated work for those who remained.

As we have seen, the labour process has been divided up into a number of separate, relatively simple tasks. This made it easier to replace full-time staff with casuals. Further pressure came from liberalisation of legal restrictions on trading hours. The department stores employed more casuals on Monday, Thursday night and Saturday morning to accommodate the new five day week roster for full-time staff. They were also becoming more attentive to peak trading hours (such as lunch-time) and the greater flexibility of casual staff. In May 1980, Myer made a particularly blatant attempt to reduce the hours of 133 full-time staff to twenty a week, the minimum number of hours for part-time employment under the shop employees award. They argued that it would allow for a better staff mix in relation to trading profits. Further, they claimed that those concerned 'would not be disadvantaged as they presumably had full-time working husbands'. After much industrial action this tactic was defeated. More recently retailers have attempted to transfer full-time staff to 35 hours a week, on reduced pay, which may represent a more gradual and cautious strategy for achieving essentially the same result—a reduction in the numbers of full-time employees and an increase in part-time employment.

One company provided figures that showed a full-time staff of 42.5 per cent and casual and part-time employees at 57.5 per cent. The latter percentage almost entirely represented casual employees—permanent part-time work makes up less than two per cent. Figures provided by the SDA placed the full-time workforce at 28 per cent, and the casual and part-time workforce at 72 per cent. A further claim, based on figures from the Victorian branch of the SDA indicated that full-time staff had fallen from 40 per cent in 1972 to 14 per cent by 1979 (Lansbury, 1980: 289). While these figures may not be entirely reliable, they do indicate the general trend.

This trend takes slightly different forms in supermarkets and department stores. The casual workforce in the larger supermarket chains comprises three distinct groups. Those employed on Thursday night and Saturday morning, including the supervisors, are juniors, typically schoolkids, both male and female. The girls are put onto 'women's work' on the cash registers, for which they are trained for a maximum of twenty hours, compared to three weeks on the earlier machines. The training consists largely of perfecting the 'mode of sale'—'greet customers with a smile, pull the rack over, left hand moves

the articles. While the right hand registers the sale, call all prices...'
and so on. The boys stack shelves or pack groceries, as well as doing
some packing in the back of the store. While the girls are under close
observation, their output measured, the boys have an easier time. They
can regulate their work by leisurely bringing in trolleys from outside
the store or slipping off to the fire escape for a cigarette. It appears to be
common for the manager to pick out a reliable male to perform some of
the routine tasks of supervision. All of this creates considerable
antagonism amongst the females.

The night fillers are now mostly senior women, as well as students
and second job holders. Although they supposedly work on a roster, in
some stores they are required to ring the manager two hours before the
commencement of work to enquire whether their services are needed on
that particular night. They are expected to make themselves available
on the four major shelf-filling nights each week, although they will not
necessarily receive work.

The third area of casual work, the daily trading peaks, is filled
entirely by married women. Many of these are long term reliables who
also fill in when the full-time staff have their days off. The situation is
only marginally better in department stores, where the same trends are
in evidence. Staff are only dimly aware of how many of their number
are casual—because casuals tend to work longer hours it is less obvious.
It is clearly in management's interest that these women continue to be
lumbered with home and child care, so that these are the only jobs they
are free to take. These casuals constantly experience the threat of
replacement. The youths are typically sacked at age 18. The women are
constantly inspected to see if their 'mode of sale' is adequate. One
company recently doubled the number of girls employed from thirty to
sixty and advised them that they may not be required to work every
week. They consider the company's intention to be weeding out all but
the fastest and most passive employees. This effectively means the
application of piece rates since people are not employed unless their
output is high enough to 'justify' the wages paid. The women further
objected to frequent sexual harassment from both male customers and
supervisors.

Some of these problems could be ameliorated by the extension of
permanent part-time work. Even the Thursday night/Saturday morning casuals could be put on a permanent basis. The SDA is pushing for
this. Unfortunately, they seem only too willing to do a deal with the
employers, allowing the continuing erosion of full-time jobs in exchange for part-time benefits. There is a danger of further entrenching
low-paid part-time work by validating it in this way. At a time when few
casuals were employed, the union allowed their conditions to deterio-
rate: before 1957 they received the full adult rate, since then they have
been paid on an age (as well as sex) basis. By 1977, when the trend

towards teenage casual labour was clear, Justice Macken attempted to moderate it, by insisting on an hourly rate based on that for 19 year olds. But it was too late. Fast food companies were specifically exempted, on the grounds that the uniforms provided, and the required use of American jargon, made these jobs unsuitable for adults. This was an close as Macken could come to an admission that the organisation of work in fast foods in particular, and retailing in general, is increasingly based on the employment of a young casual workforce.

The SDA has done little to counter this process of casualisation or the major transformations in the nature of retailing work that have made it possible. They have negotiated with employers to such an extent that they have been actually *behind* the findings of the arbitration courts. They have discouraged militancy and prided themselves on being a union that does not stand for strikes or support any on-the-job actions. Without union backing, workers in retailing have had little opportunity to organise around increased productivity, working conditions or industrial health. The development of a casual, malleable workforce is such a fait accompli that those who do seek change are starting from way behind where they should be. The SDA's new concern with 'reskilling' may be seen as too little, too late.

Working at a discount

Retailing has a much higher proportion of women workers than banking. Yet men retain all the top positions and there remains a clearcut sexual division of labour, with rationalisations as to why some jobs are appropriate for women and others for men. It is more obviously sexualised than some of the other industries. This has to do with the ways in which the buying and selling of commodities is used to create sexual meanings, still constructed around a polarity of 'masculine' and 'feminine'.

The entry of women has coincided with a massive transformation of the labour process since the 1960s. Old skills have been lost and new skills barely recognised. Feminisation has been a central part of the processes of automation and job fragmentation that we have described. At the same time, these women are tough. They resent being pushed around and they are well-placed to fight further deterioration of their working conditions. A strike of checkout operators could create havoc, given the importance of getting the goods through the turnstiles quickly. They are angry about sexual harassment from customers and male staff, and the petty humiliations around issues like dress and toilet breaks. Those in junior 'management' are beginning to see the extent to which they are exploited for that $5 a week more. As the ranks of middle management have been thinning, their prospects for moving up are narrowed. We are likely to see a clearer gap between bosses and workers and greater cynicism about the way in which 'management' is held out as a carrot, to get people to identify with the interests of the company.

As shop work comes to resemble factory work more closely, the belief that it is 'middle class' becomes harder to sustain. Working class women have few illusions about why they work—they have families to support and they need the money. Many express a working-class feminism which people too often presume does not exist. Their dissatisfaction with their working conditions is closely connected with anger about their treatment as 'girls' by management and customers.

4 Roaming around computer-land
Sex-typing in a new industry

Computers are the thing to do.... They're here to stay.... It's a safe industry. *Female trainee programmer*

Computers mean jobs—if they take jobs away they also make new ones. *Male trainee programmer*

I thought, this is terrific, I'm all for it. Anything that replaces a pencil and rubber is good. *Female administrator, computer centre*

I had been thinking vaguely about doing library work and someone said, Oh, don't do that, that's all going to be computerised. At that time my father was putting a library on computer, so that confirmed it. *Female, Staff Training, Programming*

It is not surprising that computer workers have such naive beliefs in technology as a force for progress. They are where it is all happening; the computer is the future. Notice the difference between these comments and the whitegoods workers' views of the future.

In manufacturing, banking and retailing, the introduction of computerised technology is having a devastating effect on the workforce. As one programmer recognised, 'My job is putting other people out of jobs'. The computer has been management's major weapon in increasing control of the labour process and reducing labour costs. The results are often rationalised in terms of the removal of unpleasant tedious jobs, and the creation of new interesting computer-related work. Computer workers readily adopt this ideology. The mystification of machines that occurs in industries like whitegoods is particularly apparent in computing. The environment in data processing centres contributes to this—modern windowless buildings with heavy security precautions. The computer is often locked away, inaccessible to most of the workforce. In one data processing centre we went into it was in a big glass cage that could be looked down into from a viewing area. The mystique about computer work is also maintained by keeping sections of the workforce rigidly separate, on different floors of these buildings.

However, the logic of capital does not spare those in computing. Fragmentation of work and deskilling occur here as elsewhere. And although it usually goes unnoticed, there has always been a large number of jobs in the area that were not regarded as skilled. Why these jobs are conveniently forgotten by those pushing the virtues of computer work, relates to another myth about the industry. Namely that because it is a new industry, it is not organised around gender in the 'old-fashioned' way and is open to men and women on equal terms. Yet unskilled data entry work is entirely done by women, is not seen as computer work proper, and is consequently ignored.

We want to show in this chapter that gender divisions are as central in a new industry where jobs are supposedly nonsex-typed as they are in others. The sexual division of labour is not a remnant from the feudal past that is gradually being eliminated, but is a fundamental structural feature of capitalist society. A gender analysis also brings into focus some other limitations in the ways we have thought about the history of data processing.

The sexual division of labour and the deskilling hypothesis

Of the 70,000 or more computer workers in Australia, most are employed by the computer companies or by user organisations (Beardon, 1980: 6–7). The banks and the large retailers have some of the biggest and most sophisticated computer operations. This figure of 70,000 does not include the data entry clerks, of whom there are perhaps double that number: no one seems to have accurate figures. Women predominate in this unskilled data entry section where they form virtually 100 per cent. This work is so downgraded that it is not usually thought of as part of computer work at all. Operating has been reduced to unskilled manual work but is, for various reasons to which we will return, defined as male and paid much better. Programming is supposed to be uni-sex but men predominate and women tend to be concentrated in the lower ranks of the coders. Relatively few women move into systems analysis and fewer still into management. They do, however, appear in demonstrating, teaching and consulting work, jobs that are held to be consistent with 'femininity' in that they draw, for instance, on interpersonal skills and are less directly competitive. Women still are more likely to be accepted in professional than business circles. There is big money to be made in the sale and installation of computing equipment. Of all the industries we looked at, computing is the most ruthlessly cut throat. It is, synonymously, the most macho. One of the few women in this area commented, 'The selling sphere is nasty. They just drink and leer at women all the time. Any women with sense would keep out'.

Marxist accounts of computing, as with other labour processes, have focussed almost exclusively on deskilling (Greenbaum, 1979). While there are good reasons for this, it has been done at the cost of ignoring those who are *already* deskilled, who just happen to be substantially women. To talk about data processing as a craft is already to exclude the lower ranks, who were *always* there. The first business computers were used to perform clerical functions previously done by accounting machines. Women moved from these machines to prepare the routine data for the computer. It was the existence of this army of women that enabled the programmers to experience themselves as 'free-wheeling, independent crafts people'. This is not unlike the situation in the banks where men have been able to experience themselves as career bankers because the ever increasing proportion of routine machining jobs have been done by women. In computing, the gulf between the keypunch women and other computer workers has been treated as so natural that half the labour force has been effectively removed from consideration, not even regarded as part of the same industry. They are, of course, often geographically separated, being employed by different companies specialising in data preparation. And in some cases (Ansett, Medibank), the processing work is actually sent overseas where wages are cheaper still.

Thus it is that data processing is seen as a predominantly male domain and the issue of sexual equality is reduced to a question of how women can gain recognition in this male world, or 'why do so few women reach senior positions?' We want to move beyond this framework by locating gender and sexuality as part of the historical development of the labour process in computing.

If the deskilling hypothesis leaves out one half of the workforce, can it be said to be applicable to the other? Those who have used it have had populist notions that deskilling is creating a large and undifferentiated new working class. This ignores the deep divisions and differing interests that are present even in the old working class, in areas like whitegoods. The concept does not carry over quite so easily to new 'middle class' occupations. Another problem with treating the history of data processing in terms of deskilling has been the failure to consider the class position of the programmers. While it may be true that their work has become bureaucratised and routine, this does not automatically give them a proletarian consciousness or place them in the ranks of the working class. They may have less job satisfaction, less freedom of movement and a less 'bohemian' lifestyle than they had in the past, but as a group they are still doing very well. While there was some slowing down of their salary increases in the early 1970s, since the latter part of the decade the industry has boomed and they have benefited from it. In 1978 salary increases for data processing professionals kept well ahead of inflation and came a close third to mining exploration and the upper echelons of corporate executives (*Pacific Computer Weekly*, 1 March 1979). While America recruits from England, Australia has relaxed its immigration restrictions to allow entry to six categories of computer workers (*Pacific Computer Weekly*, 21 August 1978). Because of their scarcity, data processing (DP) professionals retain considerable bargaining power over pay and working conditions.

This does not mean that deskilling as an offensive of management can be dismissed. Higher pay only serves to distract attention from the more fundamental changes. Programmers are not about to join the working class en masse but they are experiencing more shared interests. This is particularly true of the low level coders, who come in with less training and whose salary and career prospects are starting to fall behind. Moreover, supply conditions are likely to change rapidly. A 1979 survey in New South Wales indicated that while there was currently a shortfall of experienced analysts and programmers, far too many trainees were being produced to meet future requirements (*Pacific Computer Weekly*, 11 May 1979).

The early days

Why should a *new* occupation become sextyped so rapidly? We are offered the romantic image of the eccentric loner, stumbling into the field as if by accident. Women were not free to roam around computer-land, to explore new and strange territory, any more than we are free to hitchhike or travel alone without risking harassment. The field had a maths or science image. This restricted women's entry though not men's: a 1963 survey found that only 45 per cent of programmers in fact had such a background (Greenbaum, 1979: 87). It is as if the image were there purely to keep women away.

More to the point, the computer represented power and control. It was assumed that women would not understand the workings of such big machines and were fit only to 'feed' them with data. The operations area was always considered 'male', partly because the work was initially quite heavy and partly because it was closely identified with the armed forces. The first modern computers were, after all, World War II projects funded by the military. And the development of computerised technology continues to be closely linked to war.

Once an area becomes sex-typed it tends to stay that way. Furthermore, employers assume that if men and women are working side by side without supervision their animal (hetero) sexuality will break loose and anarchy will prevail. They talk endlessly about 'hanky panky' and 'Peyton Place'. Bell had resisted male telephone operators for the same reason. Management like to keep the sexes separate unless it is a controlled situation of the boss-secretary type, where it may be in their own sexual interests to have them together. The rituals that daily create masculinity and femininity must largely be enacted in single-sex groups, at a distance from each other and with a measure of tension. Hence the macho qualities associated with programmers and operators and the way this operated in group situations to freeze women out.

But women were not entirely frozen out. Particularly to some of the small computer consultancies, they were attractive because they could be paid less. In the 1950s women were typically being paid only 75 per cent of the male rate. Even today they frequently earn around $2000 less than their male counterparts in the *same* firm. Some companies also decided that women were more pliable *and* more likely to work co-operatively to solve a problem than the men, who were highly competitive. Thus the first sexual division of labour in computing was between the 'professionals' and the punch clerks. Within the 'professional' area a minority of highly qualified women were employed in subordinate positions and exploited. Eventually many of these women became restive and began to push for change.

Changes in the labour process and the sexual division of labour

From the late 1960s many more women moved into computing. What made this possible was a shortage of skilled labour. Under such circumstances sexist stereotypes get revised though never dropped. To fully understand the change we need to look at changes in the labour process and recruitment policy.

In the early period companies were willing to invest heavily in research and development. By the 1960s they sought a greater return on their money and improved efficiency. Where the first generation computers had operated clumsily on vacuum tubes and the second generation ones on transistors, IBM's System 360 heralded a third generation of streamlined and reliable 'general purpose' computers which were based on the integrated circuit. They brought in a much wider range of business users. They also marked the beginnings of more formalised distinctions between jobs: up till that time the main division was between punch clerks and professionals. The work of operators and programmers had substantially overlapped, for changes in the operating program were initially made by actually rewiring the computer. Operators needed to understand a reasonable amount about programming and programmers spent a lot of time in the computer room guiding their program through.

Now that hardware and software were clearly distinguished, a stricter demarcation could be set up. This demarcation combined with stricter security precautions to deny programmers entry to the computer room. The first step of separating conception (programming) from control (operating) had been taken and the operator's job reduced to a manual occupation. In the second step business communication was divided off from technical orientation. Thus systems analysts were employed to communicate with management and to deal with business problems;

programmers could be left to deal with the technical side. Within each of these categories a number of subdivisions developed. So quickly did this happen that in under two decades people were unaware of the origins of their jobs and assumed that these divisions were fixed, inevitable and, presumably, 'natural'.

Systems analysts have been predominantly middle class males. Their job was defined as requiring creative thinking (male!) and business skills. Since women have never been welcome at the top of the business world, they were substantially excluded. Analysts occupy a strategic position as far as knowledge of the business and the computer systems goes. This has caused management some concern about loyalty. (We found that the banks have usually dealt with this by recruiting from within the bank.) The separation of analyst and programmer was an important means of maintaining management control—programmers now have little knowledge of the business. Analysts are basically *business* people and their identification is likely to be with the company rather than with the computer industry.

The *operators'* jobs were the most rapidly deskilled as the new hardware and software increasingly took over their functions. The operators were progressively denied any involvement in developing programs. Their jobs were defined as exclusively manual so it became unnecessary for them to understand what the programs were even intended to do. Given that the heavy work also declined, we might have predicted a greater movement of women into the area. However, it has remained largely restricted to working class men. The formal explanations given are in terms of night shifts and overtime payments. To this we can add that with overtime payments the operators earn a lot of money, at times more than the programmers. They can certainly feel superior to the punch clerks and they have retained some of the glamour of working with expensive equipment. There is the same connection between masculinity and machines that we found in the whitegoods industry.

The 'night shift' rationalisation is interesting given that there are also night shifts in 'factory' areas in data processing. These are staffed entirely by women. They are usually married women, who are considered reliable for night shifts. The work is seen to be particularly suitable for them as they can do their second shift—domestic and childcare work—during the day. What is significant is that night shift areas are very clearly sex segregated because it is at night that sexual interactions could be expected. Management wish to minimise the possibility of such distractions from work. Women express a fear of sexual harassment. Female programmers were worried about the danger for any women who tried to get into the operations area. And when occasionally a women does work as an operator she is labelled a loose woman. In fact, where women do work as operators they are more likely to work with other women. The 'same sex' principle has been preserved, the gender merely reversed.

Training in operations is practically oriented and depends on learning from one's work mates. This also keeps women out since they cannot be treated as 'mates'. Sexuality is thus central in the reproduction of gender divisions by the workforce. It is also an important aspect of the reproduction of class divisions within computing.

> They're rough yahoos [operators]. We're more refined, intelligent and gentlemanly. They used to be flunked out programmers but now they've dropped the test they're just appalling. They talk like sex-starved animals. We don't mix. I have a mate who's an operator. We say g'day to each other in the pub but couldn't join each other's drinking scene.

Needless to say, this comes from a male programmer. It is a very clear expression of different masculinities associated with class differences. Working class men are seen to be closer to the animal world, 'sex-starved animals', and middle class men are 'civilised, refined, gentlemanly'. It seems possible that as the job has become more routine and limiting the operators have projected an even stronger 'macho' style as some sort of compensation and expression of their identity. They have as a group become very isolated from other workers in the field, locked in with the computer as effectively as other people are locked out.

Programming is the most complex area to assess. Women have moved in steadily to the extent that it is now claimed to be nonsex-typed, though men still predominate. How are we to explain the movement of women into this area? Is there a relationship between 'deskilling' and the partial feminisation of the area? The short answer is 'yes' but the relationship is a complex one. Feminisation certainly does not 'cause' deskilling, as many male trade unionists have been inclined to believe, and neither does deskilling automatically bring about feminisation, as we have noted in the case of the operators and in the whitegoods industry. To understand the position of women in the 'professional' areas of data processing, we need to look further at technological change and changes in the labour process. We also need to remember that while women are congregated in the lower ranks of programming they *are* pushing their way upwards.

Programming has presented problems for management. They were in the embarrassing position of not understanding what their workers did and having little control over them. They were looking for ways of measuring productivity. This was assisted by the development of languages like FORTRAN and COBOL which simplified coding procedures. It was taken a step further with structured programming. This tells the programmer what instructions to use, what logic to follow and what routines to insert into the program. While this obviously implies deskilling and a loss of control over software production, it has been popular with programmers. As an aid to systematic thinking, it has a precision and an elegance that is to be admired. But, as Kraft suggests, it has been adopted not for its intellectual virtues but to make it easier to manage programmers (1977: 59). Basically, structured programming made possible a fragmentation of jobs and the setting up of complex hierarchies. The work is controlled by the chief programmer or team leader and much of the coding work is extremely routine. That is, there is a higher proportion of support staff who come in at low levels of skill and are paid accordingly. In Sydney, the Department of Technical and Further Education is developing courses appropriate for these people.

This whole process is now going much further with non-procedure oriented languages and structured implementation. The former means that instead of telling the computer *how* to do what is required the computer itself is left to figure this out. A large number of people can now work on or review a program simultaneously. This takes away the individual's control of both how and at what speed the work is done. Management themselves have spelt it out quite nicely:

> Our latest effort will utilise a top-down approach to the extent of requiring every stage of program development to yield visible output.... What we've devised is nothing new. Henry Ford designed the assembly line in the first decade of the twentieth century. All we're doing is applying the concept to the manufacture of application programs. (*Datamation*, 1 Nov, 1978: 148)

They feel, nonetheless, that they are still in the unfortunate position that software development is not science, it is a craft and our knowledge 'is of the meagre and unsatisfactory kind' (*Datamation*, 15 Nov, 1978: 32).

> Despite improvements, the productivity of today's programmers is no more than two or three times the productivity of programmers of a quarter century ago. In the same period, the price/performance ratio of computer hardware has improved by a factor of perhaps a million.... Further, the tasks are getting harder, as we learn how to solve one class of applications we tackle harder ones. The software problem is therefore a rolling crisis. (*Datamation*, 15 Nov, 1978: 27,30).

Despite the obvious deskilling, programmers are still in a good position to restrict the controls over their labour.

What all this indicates is that deskilling is by no means a straightforward process: just as management think they have solved things, new problems arise. It is too easy to assume that they have it all their way—that they set up job hierarchies and control of the workforce is achieved. To complicate the picture, the workforce often experience deskilling as its reverse. For example, in learning new languages they believe they are acquiring additional skills. While this may be true, the new languages will eventually make the job simpler and remove the need for earlier skills. At the same time as data processing became more standardised it was also experienced as more specialised. The 'jack of all trades' (sic) gave way to new hierarchical arrangements designed to keep people locked into particular job ladders through making minute distinctions between jobs. This created the possibility of a much more complex division of labour. It was aided by a recruitment policy with different methods of selection and degrees of education being used for entry into each ladder.

As jobs and qualifications became standardised and defined, more women were recruited. The logic of this is taken to be so self-evident that no one ever stops to ask why? Partly it was because the rapid expansion generated a labour shortage, but there is a further reason. Men often become threatened by the entry of women to previously male occupations. At a conscious level this is expressed in terms of fear of competition and lowered wages. But there are other levels. Although gender is deeply engrained, it has to be maintained through day-to-day activity and is thus always in danger of being disorganised, with unsettling results. If women move into male areas, men feel their masculinity is being attacked. They prefer to keep women at a 'safe' distance (as far away as home!). Now bureaucratisation supplies *just* that distance by creating set places for people and by minimising the obligation to interact closely in recruitment, training or the job itself.

In confirmation of this, women have a preference for, and seem to have an easier time in, large companies with bureaucratic structures. Women school-leavers are certainly in no doubt that they will get a better deal in the public service, followed by the larger bureaucratic companies. In such organisations women feel that they have a chance to be compared with more people, and on a fairer basis, since there are fixed methods of appraising people and less reliance on personalities and individual impressions. This may well be false optimism in the light of what we have said about dwindling career opportunities. As we pointed out in the case of the banks, equal opportunities have been held out to women at precisely the same time as the career ladder is being dismantled. However, patriarchal control in its bureaucratic form is less daunting to women. And it frequently means that they have an easier time getting such things as maternity leave.

Equal opportunities does not mean that women go into companies on equal terms. Women who want to 'make it' have to play company politics. They must be tough while at the same time meeting the conventions of 'feminine' attractiveness. In computing they have been more likely to succeed in consulting work where, though the pressure is, if anything, higher they are separate from company politics.

Toys for the boys: sexuality and the computer

We will not understand the problems that women face in the computer industry by restricting ourselves to an economic analysis, even one that takes account of gender. Lurking behind this is the symbolism of the computer, which we have to acknowledge and attempt to demystify. We have pointed to the association between masculinity and machines. This goes back to the time when a connection with machinery was made a criterion of 'skill'. The computer is the ultimate in machines, the giant phallus. Men see it as an extension of the social power they are allocated through possession of a penis. Indeed they see it as an extension of the penis. And just as they regard their dicks both as supremely powerful and as playthings, so they do the computer. Simultaneously, they regard women as toys and as objects to have power over. All of this gets conflated in the common practice of flashing up blue movies and computer printouts of naked women on the video screens. This is taken further with the development of the home video market. The power of the look is combined with control over the image (let's play that bit again) and over the machine.

> My boss loves looking at women. He set up his office with glass windows and nice women sitting outside them. Everyone knows what they are there for. The upper management are all like that though. They have this fetish for looking at women.... And they're all so ugly. They're getting fatter and fatter from their business lunches. (Woman software worker)

Men in computing, particularly those who work for the computer companies, seem to combine a gaucheness about sexuality with an immense capacity for objectification. On the one hand they are naughty little boys with dirty pictures. On the other, they fancy themselves as the sophisticated exponents of a 'liberated' sexuality. Permissiveness, meaning *their* right to sexual freedom, is seen as central to the new technological age. They represent a worldview in which technology triumphs over everything. Technological domination and sexual domination are one and the same thing.

This is essential background for understanding why computing is so strongly 'male' and why women are having a difficult time. The 'uni-sex' image was no more than a metaphor for the 'swinging' sexuality that was supposed to accompany technological progress. After all, wasn't it the 'technological' breakthrough of the Pill that catapulted us there? Computing is, in fact, no more 'uni-sex' than Playboy. In this context, it will not be enough for women to fight discrimination, or get better access to education, important though these things might be. We have to be clear about what is going on at the symbolic level and to speak out about it.

Women programmers have an easier time in banking or retailing than they do in the computer companies. But even here they have experienced hostility and discrimination. Training is often a testing ground for perseverance. Typically, courses have about four females, and twenty males, and half the women leave.

> I had hassles with the guy in charge. You have to be interested in him. He's disliked by the women. I wasn't interested so he tried to get rid of me by saying that I wasn't progressing.

> You'd have your hand up and they'd go to the guys first. I felt like chucking it in but thought why the hell should I?

> There were three guys as supervisors. I didn't feel like asking them things. Not because they were men but because they were big. They're not little people . . . they make smaller people feel a fool when asking questions.

These women's experiences suggest an overtly sexual response to threats to masculinity. The struggle continues on the job:

> Because you're left to your own devices in programming the blokes are very slack. I get frustrated because I have to rely on others who are not efficient. . . . Men put you down all the time because they're insecure. . . . Whenever a girl makes a mistake it's always much worse than when a fellow makes one.

Another woman put it differently:

> It's terrible for men if women are better . . . and they *are* because it's basically about organisation and women are far better at that than men.

Programming is still predominantly male, and there is resistance to women coming in. One woman who had moved from the bank branches into EDP said:

> The branches were more tolerant, you had more girls to back you up. In data processing they're particularly chauvinist, and you really have to prove yourself.

In other words, banking is women's work, and computing is men's work.

Women are gradually being allowed into programming. To take our argument further, we might note that if there are a high proportion of women in the lower ranks, it makes junior males feel a lot more secure about *their* promotion prospects. Given deskilling and a decline in promotion opportunities this is important. It is, of course, in the lower level coding jobs that women are primarily located. If they go further they have particular difficulties in combining a career with private life. The long and unpredictable hours make the juggling act very difficult. They can be called out at all hours to supervise their work going through the computer or to straighten out urgent problems. To get on they need to be assertive and to make particular efforts to stand out at work. They also need to be superwomen both at work and at home. If one area doesn't get them, the other very likely will.

We mentioned previously that training is an area that women are to be found in. This has always been the case in the training of the 'process workers' as they are all women. It is increasingly so in programming, presumably because the work is becoming deskilled, and again it is women who occupy the lower levels. A woman in programming training gave us an interesting description of her job:

> It's basically supervisory. I sit at my desk and people come to me with questions, and problems with the terminals. I teach them how to use the terminals, especially how to log on and log off. I hand out courses and work out which ones people should be doing and in what order. It's more like babysitting than teaching.

It is interesting how often women describe their paid work in terms similar to their unpaid work in the home. Management of course make the same comparisons in considering certain jobs suitable for women. Has it yet dawned on them where women's superior organisational skills come from?

The future

A number of women in computing have overcome the stumbling blocks and reached senior managerial positions. They are doing so, however, at a time when the industry looks set to undergo fundamental changes which will cause an upheaval of the labour process as profound as any to date. What will make this possible is the maturation of Data Base technology and the dramatic growth of semi-conductors. The micro-processor, based on the silicon chip, makes a reality of personal computing, intelligent terminals and networks and distributed processing. The likely result is that the communications and data processing industries will merge, and the fully automated office will be scarcely recognisable. Along with this a *new* sexual division of labour is developing which looks like becoming entrenched.

In the first place, it is the end of the road for the keypunch operators, who have always been marginalised and ignored. Their work is not only arduous, repetitive and boring but is about to be phased out altogether. It may be unskilled but it too has seen major changes over the years. As the diskette replaced the ubiquitous punched card, the number of strokes per hour increased steadily to a point where it approached the physical limit. Punch or accounting machines were replaced by only three-fifths the number of key-disc stations. Now optical character reading (OCR) is being developed. It already reads a wide variety of type faces and converts them into computer understandable data. The micropad allows data to be handwritten directly into the computer. The other form of input which is being made possible is the human voice. With these developments few specialist data entry people will be required. In other circumstances it would be pleasing to see the drudgery of what management like to call the 'factory' area disappear. But what will happen to these women? They are not being retrained. It is those with typing rather than computer skills who are getting the jobs on word processors. In America some are recruited into the lower ranks of coding. In Australia this is rare. The DP women are treated as the lowest species of clerical worker. They will be expected to quietly disappear into the home, though they are the group that can least affort such a 'luxury'.

As the terminal itself becomes a computer, information can be punched in by people out in the field, by merely plugging into the nearest telephone. This is known as distributed data processing and has even wider implications for the way the work process is organised. It creates the possibility of substantially decentralising the workforce. It is cheaper for companies to establish small offices in the suburbs or to pay people to work at home. One does not have to look too far to see companies tapping the supply of suburban housewives looking for part-time employment as a cheap and flexible supply of labour. It is unlikely that these people would ever get unionised since they would work in complete isolation from each other and their productivity could be continually monitored. In Australia this is just starting in the form of small consultancies. Overheads are small and the cost of the terminals is now as little as $2000 a piece. Women at home with small children will obviously be the first to try it out, since they have nothing to lose. We are not suggesting that everyone who goes into this business will deliberately exploit women, but whatever their conscious intention, this move in taking advantage of the public/private distinction, has important consequences for the organisation of the industry as a whole.

The future is likely to see a drastic reorganisation of the labour process and of working conditions. The bottom rung of punch clerks will be phased out but the gap between management and the majority of programmers will probably widen. Some women will force their way to the top but their numbers will increase more steadily in the lower ranks. Management would like to further improve on programmer productivity and control. Management are very much on the offensive and can be expected to make new uses of the sexual division of labour in the immediate future, to achieve this.

The computer workers are not well prepared for such an offensive. Few are unionised and those that are are spread across a number of unions, all fighting for the control of the industry. The data entry staffs belong to the Federated Clerks Union. So too do some operators (for example, at the TAB) and programmers (for example, Alcan). The maintenance workers are in either the Electrical Trades Union or the Technical Services Guild (TSG). The programmers have been split between the TSG and the Association of Computer Professionals (ACPA), which have had a number of confrontations recently before the Arbitration Commission. ACPA has been through a series of reorganisations in its efforts to gain registration as an industrial union. As it is, these unions have done little enough for their members. The FCU has started looking at health problems but in a very narrow way, for example in extracting a small increase in pay to cover 'fatigue' from the VDU screens. It has not taken up seriously the issue of loss of jobs, being satisfied to let (un)natural wastage take place. In the case of the Victorian TAB workers, this meant that their weekly working hours were reduced (evenly and fairly!) from twenty to four or five. Not surprisingly many found this 'unprofitable' and were forced to resign. Yet strict limits on the hours to be spent at VDU screens might be beneficial to both health and jobs. The union has noted that people's speeds decline by about age 25 and they tend to move on, but it has not taken this up. As for retraining, the union holds the view that the only thing keeping women back is lack of initiative. No efforts are being made to assist them to take HSC or technical courses. ACPA seems to be in perpetual identity crisis about its professional status, and the role of the TSG is obscure.

The logic of the situation would suggest a need for one union covering all workers in the industry. Since this is unlikely, it is at least important that they ensure that the unions cater to their specific needs. With their ingrained sexism the unions certainly cannot be trusted to do anything about the various levels of discrimination outlined. Local struggles will have to be waged. There are signs that an organisation similar to the American Women in Data Processing will be set up soon in Australia. Women in Data Processing is very much an organisation for women on the way up. It is to be hoped that the Australian organisation will be broader in its membership and aims. It will be necessary for women to organise both within and outside the unions. Although women have made some inroads, men have already laid a strong claim to the more 'technical' jobs. There is no evidence at all that the sexual division of labour is breaking down. On the contrary, we have seen a fusion of the technological and the sexual. In a society based more and more on the computer this is a matter for concern. It has implications for all jobs, not only those in the computer industry.

5 Sex and power in hospitals
The division of labour in the 'health' industry

THE primary division of labour in health represents a sexual division in its most blatant form, namely that between male medicine and female nursing. The symbolism of the family, doctor/father, nurse/ mother, patient/child, has been used more explicitly in the definition of jobs and authority relations here than in any other industry. The increase in numbers of male nurses and female doctors has not changed the basic power relation. It has, we will argue, coincided with a shift from family modes to more bureaucratic modes of male domination. The sexual division of labour involves not only the allocation of tasks but a continuous sexual interaction which is as important in constituting gender as the interactions of private life. In no other work place are power relations as highly sexualised as they are in hospitals. Bureaucratic domination is directly reinforced by sexual power structures.

The workforce in hospitals

Our focus in this chapter is on nursing work within hospitals though this is not where all nurses work. Of the 63,000 registered nurses currently employed in Australia, 47 per cent work in public hospitals and 10 per cent in private ones (*Nursing Personnel Survey*, Vol. I, 1979: 109). The remainder work in nursing homes, psychiatric hospitals, community health centres, domiciliary nursing organisations, doctors' rooms and in industry. Our research is based on public hospitals in New South Wales.

Nursing cannot be thought about in isolation from the other categories of hospital work. It is in a shifting and constantly re- negotiated relationship with domestic and clerical work, and with the work of medical and paramedical staff.

Despite changes in medicine, illnesses, drugs, equipment and proce- dures, hospitals remained completely nurse-oriented until well after World War I. Nurses took x-rays and did the work later allocated to dieticians and physiotherapists. From the 1930s new occupational groups emerged and hospital managers took over some of the adminis- trative responsibilities that had been the preserve of the Matron. By the 1960s there was a high degree of fragmentation and specialisation both within nursing and in hospital work generally. Table 5.1 provides a picture of the occupational groups now employed in hospitals.

Table 5.1 Staff employed in second and third schedule hospitals and nursing homes in New South Wales, 1980

		Total	%
	Nursing	28 532	45.2
	Medical	2874	4.5
Other professional and technical staff	Radiology	779	1.2
	Radiotherapy	173	0.3
	Pathology	1637	2.6
	Pharmacy	410	0.7
	Other ancilliary services	4779	7.6
Domestic and auxiliary staff	Central administration and clerical	6490	10.3
	Dietary and food	5991	9.5
	Housekeeping	7511	11.9
	Laundry services	1122	1.8
	General maintenance	2834	4.5
Total		63 132	100

Source: Health Commission of New South Wales, Financial Statistic

The nursing workforce is also divided into different sections as is illustrated in Table 5.2.

Table 5.2 Nursing staff as at June 1980, NSW.

Category of nurse \ Employment sector	Second and third schedule hospitals (public hospitals)	Private hospitals
Registered nurse	49.9	54.9
Post basic students	3.3	—
Student nurses	27.0	5.0
Enrolled nursing aides	14.1	20.9
Trainee nursing aides	2.0	0.6
Assistants in nursing	2.7	18.3
Mothercraft nurses	0.1	—
Other	0.9	0.3
Total	100	100

Source: Report of the Task Force established by the Minister for Education, June 1981

The nursing workforce is extremely mobile. The *Nursing Personnel Survey* found that 48 per cent of registered nurses and 53 per cent of nursing aides had been with their current employer for two years or less. Of those respondents to the survey who were currently employed in the workforce, 66 per cent of registered nurses had left and subsequently returned to nursing; 61 per cent of these had left for family-related reasons, which included marriage, pregnancy and child-care responsibilities (1979, Vo. I: 100).

It also found that 68 per cent of registered nurses are married, and only 23 per cent have never married. These figures are striking, given the traditional image of nursing as an occupation for single women. A hospital administrator conceded that 'up till ten years ago we were unkind to married women'.

There is a noticeable difference in unemployment rates for married and unmarried nurses, 30 per cent compared to 11 per cent respectively (*Nursing Personnel Survey*, 1979, Vol. II: 184–85). The difference would be even more marked if we took into account nurses who have let their registration lapse. This points to the enormous difficultly of combining nursing work with domestic responsibilities. Long hours and rotating rosters present severe impediments to nurses responsible for childcare. Because these women have been forced to leave the workforce, hospital administrations have begun to increase part-time employment as a 'solution' to labour supply problems.

Table 5.3   NSW registered nurses 1980

Public hospitals:	84 per cent full-time; 12 per cent part-time; 4 per cent casual
Private hospitals:	62 per cent full-time; 34 per cent part-time; 4 per cent casual

Source: NSW Nurse Education Board

Part-time employment is not just attractive to administrations. With a 15 per cent loading and marginally more flexibility with regard to shifts, it is also attractive to nurses who would otherwise find two jobs impossible.

The irony in all of this is that nursing requiries and encourages mothering qualities, and yet the conditions and hours of work make it almost impossible to be a mother as well. Hospital administrations are concerned that part-time nurses might disrupt full-time ones because of their more favourable job conditions. Consequently full-time and part-time nurses tend to be employed in separate areas.

The division of labour

Considerable changes have taken place in nursing since World War II and particularly in the last ten years. Basic clerical work, domestic duties and catering have been re-allocated to other staff, while nurses have taken on new duties and functions. The development of task assignment involved the allocation of specific tasks to each nurse which she performed for the whole ward. The division of labour, however, is not straightforward and differs from one hospital to the next. What exactly is a non-nursing duty or a basic nursing duty is a constant matter of debate. The picture is complicated by the fact that nursing is a 24 hours a day, seven days a week activity whereas most other jobs in hospitals are nine to five. This means that, in practice, nurses still perform many tasks no longer defined as part of nursing. As we wish to argue, the occupational and professional status of nurses is highly ambiguous.

Nursing work includes:
1 'housework'—cleaning up and making beds. In intensive care units it would include changing ventilation tubing (three times a week), changing catheters (once a week), changing tubes and tapes and drips.
2 general nursing care—making the patient comfortable, sponging and showers, emptying bed pans, turning, rubbing backs, legs and elbows, cleaning up mouths and eyes, feeding.
3 healing functions—changing dressings, giving injections, intravenous feeding, handing out pills.
4 tests and observation—taking temperature, pulse, blood pressure, collecting urine for urine tests, doing ECGs and writing up reports on patients.

How are these tasks divided up and organised? The first two are largely performed by students and nursing aides. The latter are given twelve months training in what are seen as *basic* nursing tasks. Hospitals without either of these categories employ nursing assistants. Although assistants are cheaper than aides ($165.40 per week in their first year, compared with $180.40 per week in May 1981), Directors of Nursing are reluctant to employ them in public hospitals for 'professional' reasons. The NSW Task Force on Nursing Aides favours them being phased out in all sectors and replaced by aides (Report of the Task Force Established by the Minister for Education, June 1981). They are mainly to be found in private nursing homes.

Another category of workers who work under the supervision of nurses but who are not part of the nursing workforce are ward assistants. They perform tasks which are now defined as non-nursing and, like assistants in nursing, have no formal qualifications or training.

Ward assistants work with nursing staff, doing a variety of domestic chores, filling linen cupboards, carrying specimens, running messages, making deliveries, and cleaning pans. The extent to which they are used varies. At some hospitals, much of this work is still done by nurses, at least after hours. Westmead, a new hospital in Sydney, does not employ nursing aides but makes extensive use of ward assistants, the rationale being that nursing duties should be performed by the most qualified nursing staff and non-nursing duties by non-nursing staff. In practice, nursing staff here also perform non-nursing duties, particularly after hours.

Westmead also employs ward clerks to deal with admissions, show people around the ward on arrival, make appointments for them, take care of medical records, collect and distribute flowers and mail to patients, and take a daily ward census of bed occupancy. Ward clerks are a relatively recent introduction, and even where they are employed, nurses still do much of this work. In some places, showing the patient around the ward is still defined as patient care related and hence a nursing duty. In the case of both ward assistants and ward clerks, the sheer volume of domestic 'housework' and clerical work makes it necessary for nurses to perform some of the tasks.

Except at the Children's Hospital, nurses no longer serve food. In the last five years or so this has been taken over by the dietary aides. Many nurses would say that feeding is an important part of patient care and should not have been 'given up'. Even at the Children's Hospital, the food is now made up by domestic staff, following formulas worked out by doctors, nurses, and dieticians. For the most part, catering is a completely separate section of the hospital. Food is prepared and served on a production line basis. This reorganisation has made it possible to employ a high proportion of part-time staff, working only at peak times.

If nurses have shed tasks they have also taken on new ones. The tendency towards specialisation has meant that registered nurses have had to acquire specialised knowledge and more certificates. Clinical aspects of nursing have expanded. Doctors have delegated more curing functions so that, more than ever before, nurses are responsible for decisions about patients' treatment, previously the province of the medical profession. Officially, the rule about doctors making diagnostic decisions still stands but unofficially nurses make them. Particularly with the proliferation of medical technologies and the setting up of special units, the work has become more *technical* and skilled.

Fragmentation and specialisation are producing significant divisions within the medical workforce itself. While the specialists form a privileged elite the work of most doctors in public hospitals is likely to become more routine. The gap between these doctors and the para-medics and technicians, as well as nurses working in highly technical renal, cardiac and intensive care units, is getting narrower. New medical technology does not supersede or remove nursing skills. When the machinery goes wrong nurses use their old nursing skills. Indeed they frequently do a manual check anyway, for instance with automatic blood pressures and pulses. This manual checking actually makes the process more time-consuming, rather than less. To what extent then does deskilling apply here? The special units are analogous to the tool rooms in manufacturing in the period of mass production. Specialised skilled areas are hived off from the general production area, in this case the general wards. They represent a hyper-skilling of one side of the workforce while the other side is deskilled with basic nursing duties devolving to lesser qualified occupational categories. There are moves now to increase the area of basic nursing that nursing aides can perform, so that a clear two-tiered structure will emerge. In the wards, many registered nurses have become reluctant to do what they see as 'dirty work' and are only interested in the more technical aspects. This is very similar to the skilled machinists in production areas of manufacturing. In this case, it is women who work in the hyper-skilled as well as the deskilled areas.

The separation between skilled clinical aspects of nursing and basic patient care represents a radical break with traditional nursing values. In that this separation has only become obvious since the 1960s, nursing work is dissimilar to forms of work organisation characteristic of capitalism. Intensification of work and increases in output have usually been achieved through job fragmentation and a detailed division of labour. In this case it was originally achieved through professional dedication. Each nurse worked for long hours on little pay, to perform all 'patient care' tasks. Until comparatively recently control of the nursing workforce has been achieved through an authority structure that closely parallels family relations.

Family symbolism

In the traditional Nightingale system, nursing consisted of two functions: 'nursing the room' or hygiene, and assisting the doctor. Obedience to doctors was stressed; nurses were not to see themselves in any way as colleagues of the doctors. The organisation of the nursing occupation was crucial in the maintenance of the dominance of medical authority. Authority over all female staff was vested in the Matron. It was considered important that men not intrude on the area of discipline of female staff and an all female workforce was seen as essential for maintaining discipline. The Matron was responsible for organising nursing work, training nurses, and discipline in work and private life between which little distinction was made. The qualities of a 'good woman' that she was to look for and develop in her nurses included quietness, patience, endurance, obedience, unselfishness and devotion. Nurses were to be dedicated to nursing; it was a service for which they were not to expect monetary rewards; they lived a strict, cloistered life in nurses' homes. The Matron's position was analogous to that of an upper class woman in a Victorian household, with authority in her own sphere but subordinate to her husband's ultimate authority (Gamarnikow, 1978).

We want to consider the form this symbolism has taken in Australian hospitals in the post World War II period. We have talked to a number of nurses about their experiences; they have trained at different times, worked in different places, some are female, some male; but they are perhaps 'exceptional' in that they are all highly articulate and have spent some time reflecting on what nursing is about. We make no pretence that this is a representative sample. However, we do think that from the experiences of those we have talked to at length, it is possible to learn a good deal about the nature of their occupation. To assist our interpretation of their experiential accounts we also spent time in hospital wards observing the social relations of work.

Why nursing?

I came from a medical family and never considered anything else—all the males were doctors and all the females nurses. I was unhappy at boarding school, so went nursing. I kept wanting to give it up, but my parents made me stay to show I could stick at something . . . I have now been nursing for twenty years. (R, trained late 50s)

My mother and aunt were both nurses, so I was oriented to it. I wanted to do medical technology, but didn't get the necessary results. (M, trained late 60s)

I saw it as a way of leaving home and an awful family situation. My aunt was a nurse married to a doctor. I first tried uni. but nursing offered cheap accommodation away from home—even if it was restrictive. (N, trained early 70s)

There would be no way that I would otherwise have left home, except in an occupational setting . . . I went through three institutions: the family, the hospital, and then into marriage. (L, trained early 70s)

There were two things I didn't want to be at school—a nun or a nurse . . . I thought you had to be a virgin. (B, trained early 70s)

My father wanted me to be a teacher and was horrified when I went into nursing: you won't be paid and no one will appreciate you . . . (I, trained early 70s)

I liked the uniform and there was nothing else to do in 1957. . . . My big thing was I'd never be a secretary, imagine working in an office . . . in nursing you could move around, there was a lively grapevine . . . I've always felt that nurses were quite bright bouncy ladies . . . saw secretaries as confined compared to nurses, wearing their funny little boots and uniforms, who could stamp around and actually be physicaly strong . . . they had to teeter on high heels. That actual physical prowess was an important component of nursing . . . I always thought of secretaries as rather lower class . . . they were all working hard at getting married . . . we were independent, we were going to go overseas on our own money . . . (F, trained late 50s)

What is initially most striking about these answers to the question of 'why nursing'? is the sense of how little things had changed between the nineteenth century and the period when these nurses were training, ten and twenty years ago. Some important themes emerge from these answers. First, the experience of medicine and nursing 'running in the family'—males becoming doctors and females nurses. Family relations are reflected and consolidated in the hospital, and vice versa. This should not be taken as an indication of the class background of most nurses. It says more about the appropriateness of nursing as an occupation for women in professional, particularly medical families. F's comments about secretaries being 'lower class' is probably more representative: nursing is seen as a means of upward mobility for working class women.

Secondly, nurses experience a continuity in the shift from the family to their work situation; even if the hospital represents an escape from the family, it is another institution where the environment is restrictive. For many it was the only escape possible: nurses' homes were acceptable to parents and nursing offered financial independence which was not possible at university: 'I went through three institutions—the family, the hospital and then marriage'. Thus the second move, from hospital to marriage, may also be seen as an escape. In retrospect, some of these nurses now see marriage as no escape at all. They are back 'on the beat', as they refer to nursing work. Indeed in the process of escaping bad marriages, many nurses will opt for night duty, using their work as an escape from marriage.

The institutional continuity is not just between family and hospital. Many spoke of going straight from boarding schools, or convents to nurses' homes and experiencing little difference. Nurses' homes are less restrictive in the 1980s, and fewer nurses remain in them for long. But, in the 1950s and 1960s, the cloistered image predominated: 'Two things I didn't want to be at school—a nurse or a nun...' If some parents were happy for their daughters to go into nursing, knowing that a strict watch would be kept, others were not so happy about the demands for devotion: 'You won't be paid and no one will appreciate you'.

Finally, there is the sense that, given a limited choice, nursing is an occupation that offers women some opportunities for interesting work. F's comparison with secretarial work is interesting here. Whereas so many of women's jobs in factories, shops and offices are sedentary, nursing offered a chance to appropriate some space. It held out to women the possibility of an independent sense of self when not much else was offering for those who didn't want to just get married.

Training experiences: good nurses and good women?

I left because training was so bad. I never felt in control . . . I went through without ever learning about self-discipline. All my training was that I'd have to do certain things or I'd get into trouble. It was years before I realised that I was doing this or that to this sick patient because he or she needed it; I never saw myself as the actor in the situation . . . I was accused of being a streetwalker because my uniform was too short. . . . They wanted us to be ladies. You'd have to wear a corset and have clean finger nails. They'd teach you to set up trays. . . . It was very clear we weren't to have a thought of our own. (F)

This is coming from the woman who thought that nurses was bright bouncy ladies, and spoke of their physical prowess and potential independence.

I was anaesthetised by my training. It encouraged me not to think because thinking gets you into trouble. (B)

I lived in fear during my training . . . I'd lie there worrying that I'd done the wrong thing, waiting for the phone to ring from the night staff saying I'd done something wrong. (L)

We used to be *told* when our holidays would be . . . we used to have to write a letter to ask, could we come back from holidays . . . we were being trained not only to be nurses, but young ladies. (J)

The rigid discipline, fear of punishment, and denial of any independent thinking, together with the training to be young ladies, are the most vivid memories that these nurses have. These descriptions correspond to the situation in the Victorian household on which nursing was originally modelled. The position of trainee nurses is not disimilar to that of domestic servants. This makes sense of the apparent disparity between 'young ladies' and the stereotype of nurses being 'easy lays'. Domestic servants have to adopt the manners of those they serve, but being 'lower class' they are also prone to sexual laxity. Nurses shared this view:

There was this properness . . . no, it was a worthlessness rather than properness, which sort of fitted in much better with the easy lay . . . more like domestic servants. The properness was by very uptight ladies within the hierarchy that were a long way removed from the easy lays. (R)

And

I always felt that it was other bad girls, I didn't know quite who they were, but they were other, and probably not in our group. (F)

And

> I had a friend and everyone knew that if you touched her shoulder, her pants fell down. (S)

In the Victorian model, nurses' homes were designed to protect single girls whose work life put them in intimate contact with males, both patients and doctors. Victorian society did not deny sexuality but rather tried to keep it under tight control. Thus the nurses we spoke to found no contradiction between a rigidly authoritarian environment, on the one hand, and sexual promiscuity on the other. But it was always 'other girls' and 'everyone knew about so and so . . .'. This reflects differences in nurses' class backgrounds and positions. As R put it, the uptight ladies in the hierarchy were a long way removed from the easy lays. They are also a long way removed in terms of class position. In the traditional Nightingale system upper and middle class women could expect to make it into positions of authority; working class women remained in the lower echelons. The post World War II ethos of upward mobility deterred those who wished to move up from being associated with 'easy lays'.

If the images of 'respectable' and 'sexual' are not entirely incompatible, the disjunction between 'responsible', and 'servant' or 'child' is more difficult to make sense of.

> They treat you in one way as a child and then ask you to take on major responsibilities. (L)

> We liked being at . . . next to the uni. We just wanted some form of intellectual life, or some sort of feeling of being young, because if you go nursing you're not young, you're pitched right into it. (F)

At a very young age nurses are thrown into difficult, stressful situations, and yet, they are simultaneously being protected from them. Until quite recently, the subjects of death and sex were carefully avoided in training, and student nurses treated more like children.

What is the result of training; what kind of person is a trained nurse supposed to be? Nursing care is defined as doing for the sick person what they'd do for themselves if well. This is regarded as analogous to mothering, and includes not only the patient but other medical staff:

> A lot of people do have this carryover of being like Mum and taking care of *everything*, won't delegate. One sister even used to clean the surgeons' shoes if they left them in the change room. (F)

R spoke of a sister with an eight am start arriving at five am every morning. That's the way she was trained. R herself used to get into the operating theatre at five to get things sterilised for a seven am start when official start was six-thirty. She can't imagine this happening now.

The traditional view of the good nurse as good mother has been called into question, particularly in the context of professionalisation moves in the last ten years or so. But just how much has changed is another question.

> To be a nurse and look after people in a way that you wouldn't mind being looked after yourself does take a special sort of person . . . it's not just a job . . . I don't think nurses see themselves like that at all, they've been forced into this idea of seeing themselves as handmaidens. (B)

This comes from someone who trained about ten years ago. She sees a nurse as a 'special sort of person', but not a 'handmaiden'. A similar view was expressed by a Director of Nursing (Education):

> Nurses were originally surrogate mothers, good wives, handmaidens to doctors . . . we're not 'dedicated' any more, we're 'committed'. But nurses still won't ask about salaries. . .

Despite changes in nurses' professional and occupational status, the family symbolism is still strong.

The nursing hierarchy

> As a junior nurse I was watched at two o'clock one morning by the senior sister who saw me rinsing the thermometers three times and only wiping them twice. So she clipped up and pulled a thermometer out of a dying man's mouth and put it in mine, really quickly, screaming at me and waking every patient up saying that I had done to me what I did to others. (R)

> You had to let someone three months ahead of you get into the lift ahead of you, if the lift was crowded, you'd have to wait for the next one, and you had half an hour for lunch. So then you'd get into trouble because you'd run up those six flights of stairs and you'd be sent back to the bottom to start all over again. (B)

Third year nurses will frequently say that when they become registered nurses (or sisters), they won't treat students the way they've been treated. Inevitably 'the white shoe syndrome' or 'veil-itis' sets in. (Sisters no longer wear veils, and in some hospitals they now wear black shoes while the students wear white ones!)

> RNs [registered nurses] become bossy towards students as soon as they put on white shoes, because now they're at the bottom of another ladder. . . .
> In order to survive nurses have to behave the way they do . . . what the doctor gives to them they pass down the line to the student nurses at the bottom of the pile . . . and the patient pays. (P)

> People are authoritarian . . . it's the only way to survive in the organisation. I could see myself becoming a dictator . . . I *enjoyed* it in the end! That really scared me. I thought, I've got to get out of here or I'll be like the rest of them. (L)

As a nurse educator, P has watched nurses becoming 'socialised' into this structure of relations as they progress year by year. L was conscious of what was happening to her and realised the institutional constraints on one to fit into an authoritarian structure. 'In order to survive' suggests that this is the only means by which some agency can be maintained. This is part of the struggle for *nursing* space and control. What this struggle is about and why it takes this form can only be made sense of in the context of other power relations in the hospital:

> Nurses get at each other rather than doctors. They are made to get angry at each other by doctors' intervention and disruption. The surgeon yells at the CN [Charge nurse] she yells at someone else. Basically we aren't allowed to organise the way we do our work. The nurses might have agreed on a way of doing things—then doctors intervene. (G)

In what can be seen as a struggle between medical and nursing space, nursing staff take it out on each other. This is not some form of irrational behaviour that nurses get into because they're inherently bitchy of bossy; rather it is the hierarchical structure of a workforce which frequently feels under seige and in conflict with medicine. The response to medical authority is nursing authority:

> She was an old tartar . . . and of course that's what doctors have done all along so why shouldn't nurses be the same . . . (L)

But of course it's not the same. To return to the imagery of the family: the Matron has absolute authority in her own sphere which complements but is subordinate to medical authority.

> It's mother-daughter stuff: on the one hand caring, on the other hand, authoritarian . . . the old-fashioned matrons might have been authoritarian, but at least they cared. The new DNs [Directors of Nursing] are often just career people. (L)

Nurses have been disciplined by mother-daughter relations, particularly under the old Matron system. Nurse-nurse relations are analogous to sibling relations: 'sisters'. Nurses felt some loyalty to their Matrons even if they saw them as 'tyrants'. Some express regret at the changes in nursing administration and the replacement of the Matron by a Director of Nursing. Under the old system, a sense of solidarity among the female members of 'the family' could be produced in the face of the 'father', although the supremacy of his position was not to be questioned.

Nurse-patient relations

P often asks herself 'why do student nurses put up with the way they're treated'? The answer, she says, is that 'there's always someone beneath them—*the patient*'. If junior nurses are treated as children, then the patients are clearly babies. The care of babies is delegated to older children.

In the negotiation of space in the hospital one of the most important areas of struggle is over 'who owns the patient'. In this context nurses are primarily responsible for *patient control*. This does not necessarily conflict with ideas about *patient care*. 'Patients must submit to what is good for them, and being ill they're in no position to question.' The idea that nurses should act as patients' advocates, and the importance of patients' rights, is being emphasised now, and some nurses are acting on it. But by and large, patients are treated like children with no rights. Nurses adopt the term 'bad patient' for someone who questions or objects to what is happening. Patients are meant to be submissive. Bad patients can make the life of a junior nurse miserable. If she is not obeyed, she'll have to take the matter higher up and she is likely to be in trouble for her failure.

P spoke of a battle between the health team and the patient team. Nurses are in both, and although they are meant to be patients' advocates, the former team, in her experience, always wins. She recounted numerous stories about doctors' mistakes and decisions adverse to patients, that nurses did nothing about. 'They feel power-less.' When pressed, nurses will differentiate between what they think should be done and what they're prepared to do in these situations.

What we are suggesting here is an institutionalised hostility between patients and nurses. This is a result of the position of nurses in the health hierarchy and specifically the relation between medicine and nursing. Nurses feel that they know the state of patients' health because they are observing them constantly. Doctors come and go but they make ultimate decisions. So a patient might, as nurses see it, 'lie' to a doctor in order to get out of hospital. In such a situation, conflict between nurses and doctors is displaced into hostility between nurses and patients: 'doctors will always listen to patients and not to us, they never back up nurses'. Patients might disagree about this but it is how nurses experience it. None of this is to suggest that nurses don't ever confront doctors or resist them in ways other than taking it out on each other, or patients. They do, and we'll look at some examples in the next section.

Doctor-nurse relations

Family symbolism was meant to ensure medical authority. The tradi-tional distinction between nursing and medicine has been between curing or diagnostic functions and patient care but in practice the dividing line is not clear. Conflicts occur frequently. As it was put to us, the relation between medical and nursing space is constantly being negotiated—but negotiated along power and status lines. The doctors usually win because they have the power. However, disagreements do take place.

M cited a case when the doctor had ordered the wrong premed for a caesarian. She'd checked with the charge nurse and others and halved the dose to the normal amount but the baby was still born 'flat'. If she had not halved the dose the mother could also have died. Despite the doctor's negligence, she was in trouble for disobeying his orders. 'If you question things they can be very rude, especially the honoraries.'

When J was in a dialysis unit a patient was being fed by tubes for everything and the doctor asked her to give him a needle. She said the patient couldn't cope. The doctor said: 'You'll be in a lot of trouble if you don't do what I say'. She replied, 'I'll be in a lot of trouble if I do'. The charge nurse didn't want to go against the doctor, but knew he was doing the wrong thing. J won.

In each case the doctor had clearly made a mistake but his primary concern was the nurse's disobedience. Doctors will not often acknowledge that nurses have any skills and knowledge; their power is based on the withholding and mystification of medical knowledge and they are threatened by nurses questioning this in any way.

In the course of observing work on a ward, one of us noticed that the charge nurse had stopped running about. Her explanation was:

> I'm trying to extract instructions from the doctor. We have difficulties actually getting the orders from them. It takes a long time and a lot of hanging about. But if I don't find out now what he's deciding, it'll take even longer once he's gone. Doctors are difficult to find. (W).

This also points to the difference in the use of space and mobility between doctors and nurses. Nurses are very mobile, but they are confined to the ward. By comparison, doctors have enormous freedom of movement.

Doctor's failure to recognise that nurses 'know' anything is connected with the fact that medical 'knowledge' and nursing 'knowledge' are very different.

> Doctors don't believe us. But we know when someone is bleeding. We're *taught* observation. They will only go by tests, blood pressures . . . (E)

> I reckon if you're a nurse and you can't tell if someone's dead, there is something wrong with you—but we're only meant to say they have no pulse because we're not supposed to diagnose. (G)

Medical knowledge is 'scientific', nursing knowledge is practical. While 'science' is used as a means of maintaining control, practical knowledge and skills represent a potential challenge to medical dominance.

There is a long history of struggle for dominance between men and women in midwifery and it continues: one nurse said she couldn't bear to work in it because of the sexism.

Male obstetricians are into controlling the whole process. I only saw one normal birth in two months. They use forceps and caesarians to time the births to suit them. (N)

It's amazing how many normal births you have at night and weekends [when nursing staff rather than medical do deliveries]. (L)

I had delivered the baby before the doctor arrived. The mother looked from the doctor to me and said, 'Should I pay you, Sister?'. (M)

Relatively new aspects of nursing now being emphasised are 'promotion of patients' 'independence' and 'helping people to die'. All the nurses we spoke to had stories about conflicts with doctors in connection with the latter.

The most frequent disagreements with doctors are over terminal care. They'll say this . . . and then come and take blood samples every day, especially if someone has a rare tumour—they want them kept alive as long as possible. We say so and so is in incredible pain to get them written up for more and more morphine . . . (G)

As nurses administer the drugs which eventually kill such patients, they take responsibility for death. 'You feel pretty funny when you know that technically you've bumped off 20–25 people' (G). Several nurses expressed the view that doctors displace responsibility and guilt about death on to nurses. They see it as a failure and believe they have to go on attempting to 'cure' people right to the end. Of course they 'cure' at a distance, they 'don't think of patients as people'; it is nurses who actually relate to the patients and see them being subjected to 'painful, humiliating, life-prolonging procedures. . . . Doctors make death much worse for patients and relatives. . . . Brave nurses will administer overdoses' (P)

Sexual politics

Doctors exercise not only the power of the father but direct sexual power over nurses. Medical dominance is reaffirmed by sexual domination.

Playing the doctor-nurse game—you have to play the hierarchy all the time and the sexual component is pretty central; doctors expect you to flirt with them and find them attractive. (M)

That the work involves touching people's bodies exacerbates this. Thus the sexualisation of power relations is most pronounced in operating theatres.

There's this kind of flirtation thing going on all the time . . . 'and what have you got for us now sister'. (F)

For a start you're all running around in things like pyjamas. There are expanses of exposed thighs. Doctors hitch their jockettes up over their hipbone ... the surgeon will say 'nurse, I've got an itchy thigh'—and of course they're gowned and gloved and you have to go and scratch them—or wipe their brow when there's no sweat.... It's so grossly humiliating but you *can't* refuse to do it. (G)

A surgeon has the power to enforce sexual contact on nurses, particularly junior ones, as part of their nursing duties. Obedience to doctors can include sexual obedience.

What we have described so far is the most common experience of doctor-nurse relations but not the only one. There are significant exceptions to this pattern which suggest a more complex structuring of gender and power relations. In special units, doctor-nurse relations are more amicable and equal. First names are used and it is less formal. Nurses are more prepared to say if they disagree, and indeed doctors have to *ask* them a lot. The specialised skills and knowledge of nurses are acknowledged.

Junior doctors are by no means in the same position of power as honoraries or registrars.

The interns too are powerless in relation to the charge sister. It was a joke to send up the young doctors. Nurses have to teach them a lot of procedures ... (L)

The intern is analogous to the son—under the authority of mother/ big sister—but to be rewarded in the end by stepping into the father's shoes. Before this, they rely on nurses for practical knowledge and experience. We have heard stories about doctors being grateful for nurses' help and a year later ignoring or being rude to them. Some nurses make the mistake of thinking, 'If I don't give him hell, maybe he'll be different from the rest'. It rarely happens.

So far we have talked only about relations between male doctors and female nurses. How are power relations affected by the increasing proportions of male nurses and female doctors?

There has been a significant feminisation of the medical profession. In 1980 35.4 per cent of medical students in New South Wales universities were women (ABS Education, NSW, 1980). As graduates, those going into hospitals are not specialists but occupy lower medical positions. They do not have the 'rightful' authority that male doctors have. For this reason they are often experienced by nurses as worse than the male doctors.

Female doctors are bad news. They treat you arrogantly. I eventually had to shout at one 'treat me like a human being' ... (W)

What is significant here is that the charge nurse felt free to shout at a female doctor. This sheds some light on the arrogance of women doctors—they have to assert their position of power in a way that men don't. Their need to keep up with the men and to make it in a male world makes them 'worse'. They cannot afford to fraternise with nurses. On the other hand, their presence in an operating theatre has the effect of restraining male doctors in their sexual advances to nurses.

Another dimension to these conflicts is the movement of males into nursing. This has not happened on a large scale yet but there are some indications of the likely effects. Until the early 1970s, men were only in psychiatric hospitals, where the pay was higher and the work involved more use of physical force. They trickled into general nursing in the early 1970s and made up six to eight per cent of the first 1974 intake at Prince Henry Hospital. In 1978 males comprised five per cent of both the registered nurse and nursing aide workforce in Australia. However, ten per cent of nursing students were male (*Nursing Personnel Survey*, Vol. 1, 1979: 198). Until eight years ago, they could not nurse female patients, and it is only in the last five years that they have been allowed into midwifery.

The commonly accepted view of men in nursing in the early 1970s was that they were homosexual. Whether this is true or a stereotype of men doing women's work is difficult to establish. One Director of Nursing claimed that a majority *have* been homosexual. Some hospitals have begun to encourage the recruitment of heterosexuals to 'clean up the image of male nurses'. This change also reflects the new attractions of nursing to men. Professionalisation, changes in nursing administration and prospects of a career in a tightening labour market situation, have attracted men who might have gone to university. In fact many of them are doing a Bachelor of Hospital Administration at the same time. It is often not nursing itself, but the career of nursing that interests them. From all accounts, they do move quickly into administrative positions, many of them becoming charge nurses. 'They see it more as a career, they're ambitious and they're resented for it.' In at least one hospital senior nurses have made moves against their rapid rise to administrative positions.

Doctors' responses to male nurses are particularly interesting.

A male nurse in the operating theatre was quickly promoted up through the ranks, out of the theatre. He was given this incredible crash course to make him really capable so that he'd know all the operations we did. The surgeon would explain what he was doing in a way he never did to us ... I can remember them being really nice to him and we hated him. The best we could do was to make him out to be really incompetent. (F)

Heterosexual male nurses form part of the 'boys club' with the doctors ... (G)

Doctors generally can't acknowledge that male nurses are nurses. As far as they are concerned nurses are women *and* the objects of their sexual attention. If they happen to be male and heterosexual, then they're not nurses. They cannot be flirted with so they become one of the boys. If they're homosexual, they seem to represent a direct threat to the heterosexual power structure. They are not just dismissed as women. Again, the exception to this pattern is in special units where doctors *will* talk to homosexual male nurses. Male nurses are called Mister, as are surgeons, 'because nurse does have female connotations'. That male nurses get special treatment by doctors, angers many of the women. The presence of male nurses also produces rifts and divisions amongst female nurses. Some think that nurses also give them special attention:

> Male nurses get away with murder . . . RNs kowtow to them, see them as men not nurses . . . (P)

As in other industries where men and women are doing similar work, there is bitterness when men are perceived to be slacking, not doing as much as women. So although women will say that they like to have men working with them in nursing, there are occasions when a male nurse will attempt to boss them around, or refuse, for example, to do bed pans because it's women's work. Female nurses express less ambivalence towards gays than straights. They are seen to be more like them and they do not represent the threat to a woman's area that heterosexuals potentially do. In the struggle between medical and nursing space, male nurses siding with doctors weakens the strength of nurses.

The contradictions of professionalism

The movement of men into nursing has coincided with major shifts towards professionalism and managerialism. These derive from the development of a complex division of labour, reorganisation of the labour process and the introduction of new technologies. With the growth in size and complexity of hospitals simpler forms of family control are being replaced by more bureaucratic forms.

The separation between skilled clinical aspects of nursing and basic nursing creates the basis for professionalisation and yet ironically threatens the very existence of nursing as a distinct occupation. As doctors delegated more curing functions, and developments in medical technology necessitated more skills and knowledge, nurses pushed for further recognition of their skills. In this process an elite of nursing staff has been created who are reluctant to do shit work.

Task assignment has been the predominant form of work organisation. The hierarchy of tasks is allocated according to levels of training and qualifications. First year students do bed pans, progressing to medications in their second year and dressings in their third. In hospitals with no students, nursing aides or assistants-in-nursing do these tasks. Registered nurses take on the more complex tasks as well as supervising students and aides.

In response to this division nurse administrators and educators have begun to re-emphasise the importance of 'total nursing care' and the centrality of patients' well-being. From the mid-70s Directors of Nursing began to introduce a new form of work organisation, patient assignment, the ultimate aim of which is to reunify nursing tasks. With patient assignment each nurse is assigned six to eight patients for whom she performs all tasks. The basic philosophy is that this results in better patient care through greater familiarity with patients' needs. It requires greater commitment from nurses and necessitates their understanding a range of different machines and procedures. Although it is more difficult, the work is more varied and seems to provide greater job satisfaction. It could be seen as the nurse administrators' answer to Volvo's worker participation.

How does this work out in practice? It usually takes the form of team nursing and is still combined with task assignment. Wards are divided in half with a registered nurse as team leader of student nurses and nursing aides. The team members are assigned either tasks or patients or some combination of both. The extent to which patient assignment can be practised is limited by the current high patient/nurse ratio. The presence of students on the wards also presents problems since they can hardly be made totally responsible for patients. In one hospital, it has been introduced in a ward staffed by part-time nurses. There are no students here and no nursing aides as the DN considers their use to be incompatible with the system. Concord Repatriation is the only hospital in Sydney where patient assignment is practised on any scale. They have also introduced the most complete form, primary care, in an oncology ward where there are no students. Each registered nurse is responsible for total planning of care for several patients from admission to discharge. The major problem in implementing patient assignment is the legacy of task assignment and the extreme division of labour that has developed. Where a combination of both systems operate there is often confusion about who does what, which can, ironically, result in *less* patient care. A patient might have their pulse taken three times and no change of dressings. And the tendency to offload 'dirty work' onto others is very strong. Some registered nurses want basic nursing redefined as non-nursing. As one Director of Nursing put it to us, 'the structure discourages the total patient care view!'. This DN emphasised the need to retain nursing as a whole, not only for the sake of patients but because there is a danger that there will be *no nursing* left. She predicted that increasingly functions will be shed to other occupational groups, with nursing aides at the bottom end and technical, specialised staff at the top. 'Someone can look after the plumbing and someone else the embarrassment about the plumbing.' What this points to is an occupational and professional crisis in nursing. How is nursing to be defined, what occupational space does it fill and what is the status of nurses vis-à-vis other occupational groups?

Patient assignment can be seen as a progressive move for both patients and nurses. However, it depends very much on the context in which it is implemented. In the event of student nurses moving to Colleges of Advanced Education or universities much patient care could be provided by less trained people, co-ordinated in teams. More nurses aides could be used with clearer job definitions. Thus patient assignment in itself does not safeguard against a rigid division of labour and deskilling of nursing work.

This points to some problems with nurse education. Although there has been considerable debate, and nurse administrators and educators are not unified in their views on the matter, most now want tertiary education for nurses. If and when this will happen is still not clear. Nurses are the only members of the health team who do not have tertiary qualifications and they want parity with medical and paramedical staff. They want their skills properly recognised. As one Director of Nursing put it, 'It's not for the content that nurses should have tertiary education but the status—and it must be university. Physio's aren't treated the way nurses are by doctors.' While this is a logical response to the relatively powerless position nurses have been in, it would represent a double–edged gain for the occupational group as a whole. One nurse said, 'I would hate to see nurses professionalised out of nursing'. The move to tertiary education is quite compatible with and is likely to compound the tendency towards deskilling/hyperskilling. There would be a highly qualified elite and a second large tier of less qualified nursing staff. The latter would quite likely be people who, under the apprenticeship system, would have made it into nursing but with higher educational standards required would be debarred from it. This is not an argument against tertiary education so much as suggesting the need to think about it in the broader context of the division of labour in hospitals, and particularly in the context of whose interest will be served in the long run. Cost has been one of the issues in the debate. The move to tertiary education would displace training costs from the hospitals even if they lose a cheap student workforce. They have lost some of this already, with the increased number of hours spent in the classroom. A two-tiered structure, with a higher proportion of less trained people represents a cheapening of the workforce, even if the better qualified nurses were able to command a higher income.

The boss nurse doesn't wear a uniform

Professionalisation has not just related to clinical nursing. It has also had an effect on nursing administration. Changes in uniform have signified changes in nursing administration and methods of control of the nursing workforce. With the shift from Matron to Director of Nursing, the boss nurse stopped wearing a uniform. As an aside, one of the most striking features of the authority structure and division of labour in hospitals is the uniform hierarchy. Changes in authority relations in nursing have always been marked by changes in uniform. For example, nurses in the early twentieth century had an off-duty uniform. Where someone now stands in the hospital hierarchy is immediately identifiable by the colour of their uniform. For example, ward assistants will be referred to as 'the brown ladies' and dietary aides as 'the yellow girls'. Changes in forms of supervision began when nurses took off their veils. Directors of Nursing were not to be identified as nurses but managers.

The break with the Matron system took place in the 1960s when nursing administrators began to introduce changes very similar to those proposed in the Salmon report in Britain (Carpenter, 1977). Matrons wanted a new image: business efficiency. They had progressively lost status in hospital administration and were looking for parity with other administrators. Matrons' weekly ward rounds were discontinued as 'unprofessional' for managers. They were concerned that authority be derived from their position in an organisation, rather than as the female head of a household. Principles of modern business management were to be applied to nursing administration. Supervision was not to be conducted by straight disciplinary methods any more. In short, control was to be exercised less by the direct use of family symbolism, and more by bureaucratic means, with formal hierarchies and a clear division of labour.

The shift from Matron to Director of Nursing has not in itself led to major administrative changes. These have resulted from other developments like the sheer growth in size of hospitals and changes in the organisation of nursing work. The co-ordination of activities at the ward level has become more complex, particularly with the development of a range of paramedical activities and new occupational groups. Nursing staff are responsible for co-ordinating different groups of workers, paramedical staff and patients. Charge nurses (CNs) supervise all nursing staff on the ward; they roster and allocate staff, oversee nursing practice, back up team leaders and organise in-service programs.

In some hospitals, they are responsible for budgets which are worked out at the ward level for the use of equipment and for monitoring stock. To be a charge nurse is the first step on the career ladder, and there is pressure on them to develop formal managerial skills. In turn, they are responsible to an Assistant Director of Nursing who oversees several wards, making decisions about work reorganisation and negotiating with the Director of Nursing over staffing matters. Despite the efforts to upgrade nurses' managerial status, DNs are still paid less than others in equivalent administrative positions in hospitals.

There is some tension between the professionalism associated with clinical nursing and what has been described as managerialism (Carpenter, 1977: 188). The career path is via the administrative ladder and yet nursing skills are developed and practised at the ward level. After three certificates there are no further pay rises for clinical qualifications, but many will say they want to do nursing not clerical work or administration. With increasing workloads and insufficient nursing staff, conflicts between sections of the nursing workforce will become more apparent. Administrators have to get more out of people who are already overworked; while nurses, concerned about their professional standards, feel that they are not able to give adequate patient care because of the pressures on them.

In the traditional system, immediate control and discipline of the workforce was maintained by the all female hierarchy. This ensured that the ultimate authority of the male medical profession was not threatened. With the shift to business management some men have moved in. This has not led, and is not likely to lead, to any threat to medical authority as they are co-opted as *men*, or at least the heterosexuals are. If these male nurses succeed in getting powerful positions in nursing, the dominance of female nurses by males will no longer be indirect, and men will be in immediate positions of power over them. Nursing may no longer be an all-female occupation, but there will still be a strong sexual division of labour. The administrative/clinical division is potentially also a male/female division.

Conflict and resistance

Increasing nursing skills, knowledge and decision-making can threaten medical authority. Whether or not they do depends on how the relation between medical and nursing space is renegotiated. For example, where patient assignment has been implemented in a more complete form, there has been some hostility from medical staff. Doctors previously made decisions and delivered orders through the Charge Nurse. With patient assignment they are required to consult each Registered Nurse responsible for individual patients. They don't like this: 'They prefer nurses to be, and still see them as, handmaidens'. This suggests that the division of labour within nursing, and the way in which nurses organise their work can have a significant effect on power relations. The initial struggle is over the ability to organise work at the ward level; and in this, nurses have both the medical and nursing hierarchies to contend with. On the other hand, special units are examples of the potential containment of highly skilled nurses. They are separated off from the rest of nursing work in much the same manner as tool rooms in manufacturing in the 1950s, and with the same results. The workforce in these units are hyper-skilled in relation to the rest of the workforce and work quite amicably with medical staff. They have the knowledge to challenge medical authority, but generally don't because of their privileged position in relation to the rest of the nursing workforce.

The push for professionalisation could result in nursing being defined narrowly and technically, and the processes of hyper-skilling and deskilling extended. The other danger is that the reunification of tasks will be pushed for under the ideology of a return to the old values of nursing. Patient assignment nursing looks to be the most progressive form of work organisation, providing reunification in a form that can disrupt traditional doctor-nurse relations.

If patient assignment represents a potential challenge to medical authority at the professional level there are signs of resistance at the personal level.

> You were seen as copping out if you got off with doctors—top nurses wouldn't do that. One in our group did—easy affluence. (L)

> It is the closest thing to an insult to other people you work with if you go out with a doctor.... Doctors aren't privy to all the private rituals of nursing. It's difficult to struggle with a doctor if one of the nurses is going out with him. (G)

The hostility to nurses having sexual relations with doctors is quite strong. They are seen to be 'letting the side down'. This seems to be at odds with the popular view of nurses, and indeed many nurses do still marry doctors. However, this hostility does suggest some resistance to doctors, an attempt to close ranks on them even if it also involves another form of nurses turning against each other.

One nurse referred to the power struggle between the official and unofficial health teams. The official one comprises the doctors, physiotherapists, occupational therapists and charge sister. The unofficial one leaves out the doctors. No one will stand up to doctors in the context of the official team but, in the unofficial one, someone will demonstrate hostility to doctors' decisions.

This often takes the form of 'tea room' hostility. We were told that nurses do make decisions. 'Patients are managed quite subversively all the time.' For example, if an old cancer patient has a cardiac arrest nurses will 'fail to notice', and notify doctors too late for resuscitation. An enormous burden is put on young staff making such decisions but it must also give them a sense of power in a situation in which they are meant to be powerless.

Nurses will use words like power, conflict, struggle. While such nurses may not be the majority, it does indicate that the experience of conflict is there, even if it is negotiated in different ways. It is also true that doctors are often threatened by the expanding domain of nurses, and the new skills and knowledge they acquire. Doctors cannot just rest assured in their position of power—it has to be constantly reaffirmed. Anger at nurses' failure to carry out instructions, and the enforcement of sexual rituals, are both part of this process.

The power and standing of the medical profession is not as inviolable as is usually assumed. If the aim of professionalisation of nursing is achievement of equity in pay and status, there may be other means of challenging the position of medicine. More emphasis should be placed on the deprofessionalisation and demystification of medicine. All other health occupations demonstrate hostility towards medicine and this makes for potential solidarity. The notion of real equality in decision-making in the health team could be pushed in this context. Nor is the medical profession united. The Doctors' Reform Society publicly challenges the medical establishment over a range of issues: the privileged position of doctors, over-servicing, the politics of medicine, the shift in health from the public to the private sector, and inequalities in the health care and insurance systems. There are signs that medicine is under seige. There is a loss in public confidence in doctors, and increasing acceptance of alternative medicine. The proliferation of technologies and tests in the name of diagnosis, with frequently no diagnosis, let alone cure, being delivered, has had an effect on public confidence. The report of the NSW Public Accounts Committee which recommended the abolition of fee-for-service has provoked a strong reaction from the AMA. Their threats of strike action to prevent 'socialised medicine' suggest that some sections of the profession feel under threat (*Sydney Morning Herald*, 7 April, 3 May 1982). Justifying fee-for-service in terms of 'the traditional doctor-patient relationship' wears thin given the reality of hospital relations. The federal government is currently conducting an inquiry into fraud and over-servicing by doctors (*Sydney Morning Herald*, 26 May 1982).

The history of nurses' unions is one of tension between industrial and professional consciousness. State unions were originally formed in the 1920s and 1930s, in most cases in conjunction with the state branches of the professional body, the Australian Trained Nurses' Association (ATNA). They were pushed into forming trade unions by the formation of other unions in the health area, such as the Hospital Officers' Association and, in Queensland, a rival nurses' association that was concerned only with industrial matters (Hobbs, 1979: 88–89; Law, 1980: 206). There has been continual debate within the unions over the legitimacy of nurses demanding higher pay and shorter hours. Some, but by no means all, have seen this as going against everything the profession stood for. Since World War II the industrial consciousness has become steadily more predominant. In 1955 nurses in NSW marched over pay claims. The no-strike principle held by the unions has at times been broken. This has become particularly apparent in the last few years. In 1981, the membership of the Victorian branch of the Royal Australian Nursing Federation (RANF), which has now become both the professional and industrial body in all states except NSW, voted against a no-strike clause in the constitution. In NSW in 1981 and 1982, nurses have been on strike and marched over cuts in health expenditure. In the context of worsening conditions and increasing work loads, professional consciousness might not be in contradiction with industrial consciousness, and possibly encourages industrial action.

The Nurses Reform Campaign which formed in NSW in the context of the 'fight the health cuts campaign' has successfully mobilised the nursing workforce. In the recent Nurses' Association elections they won the two top executive positions. In office their focus of attention will continue to be the health cuts.

In the context of struggles against the state and federal governments it is easy to lose sight of the complexities of the power structure within hospitals. Despite the shift from family to bureaucratic forms of control, gender continues to be a central organising principle. Unless this is recognised there is a danger that popular front struggles will benefit only the most privileged sections of the workforce. Nurses are well aware of the sexual power structure although resistance has largely been on an individual, unorganised level. In the long run we want not only to preserve the existing system against cuts, but also a radical transformation of the health industry. This will involve changing the relations between medicine and nursing, and with it the relations between men and women.

6 The labour process of consumption
Housework

She spreads before him, like a rug, the drudgery of her days, long, narrow days with mealtimes stretched across them inflexibly, like iron bars, days filled with dust and drainpipes and infinite numbers of lemon tarts. (Cunningham, 1981: 51)

Walking down the street with her suitcase, she had even been glad to leave her children. Why should she have been poked into a house, mopping floors from daybreak to sunset, while the paint was drying on her unfinished masterpiece? Because she was a woman, and they had said to her, you have to have this job, and you are forbidden another, and no man will help you; now get to work. It was so unjust, she wanted to murder all men, to march on authorities until the juice ran from their wounds, and to lock them in domestic residences with whole armies of babies, and nappies to change. In rebellion, on behalf of all women, in fury, she marched from the house she had cleaned over and over again in the same places in the same way, which forever again dirtied, the scene of so many useless gestures which in no way had benefitted posterity or left a mark of any description. (Townend, 1981: 102)

SUCH was the nature of housework forty years ago. But it has changed, you will say. Smaller families mean that women no longer spend half their lives changing dirty nappies—and don't they use disposable ones now? Men take a share of child care and domestic tasks. New technology has make housework lighter and less time-consuming. From gas and electricity through to refrigerators and washing machines, food processors and home computers, it is widely believed that the housewife's lot has become progressively easier. The Myer Report on *Technological Change in Australia* was ecstatic about housework as the model for what new technology could achieve.

> More than any other sector, Australian households have been the subject of what can only be described as dramatic technological change throughout the decades since 1945. Many of the technologies have been labour-saving and have reduced the amount of work required, usually by the housewife, to maintain home and family. In doing so they have significantly improved the material comforts of most Australian households. (Vol. II, 1980: 445)

Despite their enthusiasm the Commissioners did not bother to investigate housework very seriously. In fact they devoted less than four pages to it in their report. Perhaps the optimism of the conclusions is related to the thinness of the research.

In this chapter we contest such claims, as based on some fundamental misconceptions. Technological change in the area has indeed been dramatic but it has *not* reduced housework. What we have seen is a major shift from housework as production to housework as *consumption* activity. When we think of consumption we tend to think first of all of its end point: eating the dinner rather than buying, preparing or clearing away after it. These other facets are invisible in the same sense that women's services are so often invisible or underestimated. Consumption involves not only the 'using up' but the acquisition and transformation of commodities. In a mass consumption society these tasks have expanded. In addition, consumption has taken on emotional and sexual connotations as the arena of personal fulfilment and individual meaning. Precisely because it is *not* production it is trivialised and despised. It is allocated mainly to women, who are supposed to do it for love. It is frequently treated as 'leisure' activity rather than 'real' work because the *formal* organisation and structuring of time of the workplace are absent. How the housewife's time is structured, and whether or not it is experienced as 'free time' are questions that need to be taken up.

While we are reluctant merely to relabel everything we do as 'work' it is important to realise the centrality of these activities to the system of 'consumer capitalism'. Although there is some debate about the extent to which men now share shopping, housework and childcare, most of this work is still done by women, whether they are married or single, and whether or not they are in the paid workforce. Studies of husband and wife interaction indicate some variation in allocation of tasks, but there are areas that are virtually exclusively the wife's (ironing, cooking, washing), some predominantly the husband's (household repairs, mowing lawns) and others in which both might participate (shopping, washing up, childcare) (Harper and Richards, 1979; Bryson, 1975). In the general sexual division of labour women are allocated the primary role of wives and mothers, regardless of what else they may do, and men, the role of breadwinners. The consequence of this is that even if men do help with some work it is assumed by both women and men that women are *responsible* for housework (Oakley, 1976: 92). Women who work are acutely aware of the fact that when they leave work they have another job to do at home. The above-mentioned studies found that whether or not the wife was in the paid workforce made little difference to the division of labour within the home. It can, however, make a difference to the power relation within the home, given the connection between money and power. For women who are not in the paid workforce, maintaining the traditional division of labour in the home may also be an important means of controlling some space.

It is not only that the sexes have different primary spheres. Most men and women live in the two worlds of production and consumption, public and private life. *Both* make a sharp distinction between home and work but their ways of relating the two are necessarily different. This, we will argue, is fundamental to the split and to the continuance of the sexual division of labour.

While it is true that new technologies have improved the conditions of work in the house, it cannot simply be assumed that they are labour-saving, or that they are developed for that purpose. As with other industries, we must put technological change in the context of structural change and the labour process. The logic of capital does not operate in the same way here that it does in the others. Whereas labour-saving is a basic imperative when profits have to be maximised and labour costs cut, it is not when the work is unpaid. It is ideologically important, however, as a means of selling household appliances. The indications are that new technology and new products do not reduce work but impose *new* consumption activities. Far from being liberated, women actually spend more time on housework than in the past.

Consumption work

In previous chapters we have discussed changes in the production and retailing of commodities since World War II. Commodities are also consumed; but it would generally not be considered obvious to discuss changes in the labour process of consumption in a book about work. Yet changes in the structuring of consumption activities have necessarily gone along with changes in production and retailing. Despite the illusion of free choice, the world of consumption is as structured and controlled as that of production; and like the production sphere it contains fundamental contradictions.

The nineteenth century had already seen a big increase in domestic servants, and particularly *female* domestic servants, to meet the consumption capacities of the new 'middle class'. In the twentieth century the growth of mass consumption created an urgent need for labour to manage it. As a result women as a whole were transformed into what Galbraith describes as a 'crypto-servant class'. This was rationalised as part of their natural capacity for loving and caring. Thus, says Galbraith, 'Her service to the economy hitchhikes on her sense of duty and her capacity for affection ... with women assuming the tasks of administration, consumption can be more or less indefinitely increased' (1973: 36). There has been a growing uniformity of women's experience, at least in so far as women of *all* classes are occupied with consumption activities around their own homes, and the associated relational skills have become a defining characteristic of femininity. From about the 1890s the word 'lady' began to lose its strong class connotations. As it did so the new term 'housewife' came into use as a cross-class term that reflected this new reality (Gilding, 1982: 68). 'Lady' then came to be used as a euphemism for 'woman'.

As capital removes production from households, it also expands market relations and increases the necessity of *purchasing* the means of life. Thus *shopping* takes up a higher proportion of women's time than it used to: according to one study it takes one full day a week compared with two hours in the 1920s (Vanek, 1977: 116). And it is now a very different experience. Structural changes in the retail industry have affected not only the work of retail workers but also that of shoppers. Much of the work previously done by the former is now done by the latter. The housewife searches the supermarket shelves, selects items, fills the trolley and, usually, transports the goods home.

Shopping in the 1950s was still closely related to women's 'productive' skills in the home. Basic ingredients were bought with the knowledge of what they would be turned into. Relations with the grocer, greengrocer and butcher revolved around a knowledge that would be expressed in the buying process. Not only did men not have this knowledge but they did not want it—it was women's work. The rise of the supermarket in the 1960s, and with it the increased use of processed, pre-prepared and frozen foods has led to a loss of the old productive skills and cooking knowledge. (Even domestic science and home economics teachers whom we have spoken to, hold this view.) In the process, shopping has become separated off from other household tasks. Although it involves more time and work it has, in a sense, become deskilled.

This potentially opens it up to men. As a personnel manager in retailing put it: 'The modern person doesn't want to talk to the butcher about cuts of meat'. Men can go into a supermarket and pick up standard items without it bearing much relation to traditional women's work. And they do not have to demonstrate their knowledge, or lack of it, to anyone. This might even be a way of asserting some control over an area that has traditionally been left to women, namely, what the family eats. The other aspect of supermarket shopping that makes it less 'unmanly' is the car. Because of the centralisation of shopping, people are most likely to drive to the shopping centre. Family groups are now a common sight, especially on Thursday nights and Saturday mornings.

This is not to say that men have taken over any substantial responsibility for shopping and budgeting. On the contrary, shopping has become more central to the woman's domestic responsibilities. Her value as housewife and mother is reflected largely in her success as a *shopper*. The onus is on women to get value for money and this involves attention to detail. The manager of a carpet department, who has been in the industry for decades, says he really has to know his business to contend with them:

> A husband might be asked to look but not choose. The women are the ones who do the talking. . . . You'd be surprised how much women know. They shop, shop, shop . . . really research it before they buy.

The time spent on marketing and record-keeping has actually increased. Take freezers, for instance. Seventy-five per cent of Australian homes now have freezer fridges and one-third have separate freezers (*Australian Financial Review*, 18 May 1982). These were supposed to decrease shopping time, by enabling bulk purchases to be made, but have frequently had the opposite effect. Apart from being a nuisance to defrost, they oblige the housewife to put more time and energy into bargain-hunting. While the centralisation of shopping centres and services may make distribution more efficient, it is at the expense of the housewife's time, the time she must spend travelling between centres, or waiting in queues for services which once came to her. She might have the illusion of 'being her own boss' but her hours are determined pretty stringently by the need to fit in with other people's schedules. If she does not have access to a car, or her husband will not 'take' her shopping, she is severely disadvantaged. She must either shop locally and more expensively, or as in Sydney's outer western suburbs, where there are few local shops, rely on a bus service which might operate once every two hours.

But the housewife is not simply buying goods and services. As it expanded to fill more time, shopping took on a symbolic significance. This points to the links with advertising and to the increasingly central place given to sexuality in ascribing meaning to our lives. Advertising offers us the chance to complete our sexual identities through buying commodities. Shopping is never merely economic, but very much to do with our expression of, even construction of, ourselves as feminine or masculine beings. This works differently for men and women. It is well-known that women make 80 per cent or more of consumption decisions, or at least implement that many. Consequently a great deal more advertising is directed at them. Secondly, while advertisers do stress the virility of male products it is rarely claimed that the product is essential to masculinity. Rather the stress is on the fact that the product is compatible with it. With women the advertising is directed at her need to please . . . husbands, boyfriends, children, even the dog and the cat. The attractions of clothes and makeup are of a different order from those of refrigerators or vacuum cleaners, though this distinction is blurred in some recent television advertising:

> GE's new modern kitchen collection—the height of fashion and what every modern kitchen should be wearing.

Both kinds of goods have a place in the construction of femininity: the first through self-adornment and the second through being a good wife and mother, taking care of home and family. Women are vulnerable in so far as we depend on the approval of others, particularly men. Shopping then becomes substantially about the purchase of love and approval and the construction of an appropriate self-image. As Berger puts it, 'the publicity image steals her love of herself as she is and offers it back to her for the price of the product' (1972: 134). Women have to shop not only on their own behalf but on behalf of their families, with whose needs they identify almost as an extension of themselves. Particularly notable is the development of separate children's markets. To be a 'good mother' now includes creating children in an appropriate image by consuming on their behalf. Australia's leading locally-owned petfood company is mawkishly labelled 'Luv' and we are told that the housewife 'wants a product that's going to be a *treat* —her dog will love her more if she buys that product' (Whiteside, 1978). Such are the binds of contemporary shopping! This is of course the advertisers' view and we should be careful not to assume that it corresponds to women's experience. Although advertising does work in unconscious ways, drawing on particular aspects of femininity, it is also the case that women view shopping as work and pride themselves on having good economic sense about it. It is nonetheless true that commodities have taken on an erotic significance and we experience them as offering to complete our sexual identities. Advertising does not con people in any simple way so much as mediate our new relation to commodities (Game and Pringle, 1979: 10–11).

The central point being made so far is this: new technology displaces many productive activities from the home and into light industry (clothing, textiles, food processing and so on). It also makes many household tasks easier (washing, ironing, cleaning, cooking). At the same time it is part of the development of a new sphere of consumption work. As is particularly clear in the case of shopping, this involves levels other than the directly economic. The consumption sphere is organised around (hetero) sexuality, around a supposed complementarity of masculine and feminine. This affects all areas of consumption and also feeds into the construction of gender-identity elsewhere. Women's experience as consumers and consumed carries over into the workplace where they are treated as sex objects. The 'sexualisation' of our everyday lives has added new dimensions to the sexual division of labour just when the pre-conditions were there for its demise.

The transformation of housework

It might be thought that with this growing emphasis on the *purchase* of commodities, 'readymade' goods, the work actually carried out within the home might have been reduced. This has not been the case although there has been a shift from what might be loosely called productive work to work associated with the transformation and servicing of commodities. New technology in the home has contradictory effects. While it has removed a lot of the heavy work it has done little to reduce work frequencies and in some cases has created new forms of drudgery. For instance, no aspect of housework has been lightened so much as laundry, yet time spent on it has actually increased (Vanek, 1977: 117). Women can now be expected to wash clothes daily instead of weekly. While the whitegoods factories churned out washing machines for every Australian home the alternative possibilities of laundries and laundromats have remained very limited. And since the value of household work is not clear, non-employed women feel pressure to spend long hours at it to ensure that an equal contribution is being made. A survey of use of time involving 1500 people in Albury-Wodonga and Melbourne, conducted at Griffith University, found that women who used time-saving devices made up for it by working longer on another job or by cleaning more often. When time required for cleaning and servicing the gadgets, ringing up for repairs, and buying spare parts, is taken into account, there is no time-saving effect (*Sun-Herald*, 12 March 1978).

As in the production process, technology has resulted in housework being divided into a number of separate, routine tasks and has removed the old craft knowledge. While some new skills have been acquired the overall impression is one of deskilling. Cooking, for example, involves combining constituents that have already been processed to such a degree that their origins are now obscure. Woolworths report a decline in the sale of some convenience foods because, they say, the housewife does not want *everything* done for her. Cake mixes used to require only the addition of water. Now they will add an egg, 'so that she feels she is doing something'. This indicates the extent of the acceptance of consumption as a way of life, the superiority of the bought over the home-made. Market research for John West Foods in 1981 found that convenience foods are not only widely accepted but are also felt to be of better quality and tastier than fresh foods because the best manufacturers were fussier than the local greengrocer. Canned foods, including fish, meats, fruits and deserts are used not only for family meals but for entertaining (*Australian Financial Review*, 24 August 1981). In the last year the frozen food market has expanded by 17.4 per cent in sales (*Australian Financial Review*, 18 May 1982). Activities like baking bread and cakes, bottling fruit or making jams are still admired but are no longer seen as essential housewifely skills. By way of illustrating this, Paul Fine notes that many American women operate on as few as seven basic meals. They are not taught to cook by their mothers but only learn by trial-and-error after marriage. The family becomes accustomed to a few basic dishes and great pressure builds up to keep within this safe framework (Fine, 1971). It seems likely that similar trends are operating here, and that the 'domestic science' training that many working class girls receive at school has little impact. At the same time, because of the greater range of foods constantly available, women are under pressure to create more elaborate meals and more frequently. Recipe books have never been so popular and those explaining how to make very ordinary foods look 'special' are widely advertised on television. Advertisers have jumped onto the bandwagon with the introduction of the telephone recipe line. This was pioneered by the Egg Line and has since been taken up by the manufacturers of processed foods including Maggi, Vacola and Australian Canned Fruits (*Sydney Morning Herald*, 3 May 1982). While refrigeration makes life easier it too raises expectations enormously. Gone are the days of corned beef and boiled potatoes. The microwave oven creates the possibility of serving up different meals at different times to individual family members.

Such are the 'liberating' effects of technology. There is certainly no guarantee that it will release women from domestic chores. On the contrary, there are signs that it functions as an *alternative* to breaking down the sexual division of labour, for example, by removing the work *he* used to do in the home. Earlier in the century, gas and electricity relieved him of the burden of chopping wood. When *she* is given a rubbish disposal unit and a dishwasher, he relinquishes any responsibility for washing up or putting out the rubbish while she gains the extra servicing work (Bose, 1979: 299). Lighter paints and do-it-yourself kits sold in supermarkets have meant that she has taken over a substantial area of household repairs, once 'his' domain (Middleton, 1957: 120–24). Lawnmowers are now being given as Mothers Day presents for 'liberated' women! Thus, any moves towards men sharing the housework are more than counterbalanced by the reduction of their own 'separate sphere' of domestic responsibilities. This has been transformed by new technology and what remains is now shared by women.

Here is a case of the anomolies we have spoken of in the rationalisations for a sexual division of labour. Recall the whitegoods industry where the new machines were beyond the understanding of women. The machines being produced by these machines, dishwashers for example, once located in the domestic sphere, are ostensibly beyond the capacity of most men to operate. To take the comparison a step further, household technology embodies a form of technical control analagous to that in manufacturing industry. Old craft skills have been replaced or incorporated into machines. Women are locked into work stations, homes, operating and servicing these machines. Such control will be extended with the potential use of home computers. The use of these for shopping and leisure will increase the isolation of women in the home.

The emotional dimensions of housework

If we saw housework as 'productive' we might have expected it to become more specialised, less time-consuming and less emotionally involving as 'rationalisation' procedures were applied. The reverse has been true. Housework in middle and even upper class homes has become *less* specialised. Where it once might have been divided between a cook, butler, housemaid, parlourmaid and nursemaid, now all these functions are usually performed by the one person. There has been a loss of managerial categories among homeworkers; since house-wives are their own servants. Exhortations to 'efficiency' ring hollow when worker and manager are one and the same person. Technology usually reduces staff levels. In the twentieth century the number of house-workers has increased substantially with the extension of single-family dwellings, whether owned or rented, and housework came to be performed in working class homes which could not previously afford the luxury.

As it became fragmented and deskilled, housework took on an emotional weight apparently out of proportion to its own inherent value. Thus laundering became not just laundering but an expression of love; cooking and cleaning were regarded as 'homemaking', an outlet for artistic inclinations and a way of encouraging family loyalty; changing nappies was not just a shitty joy but a time to build the baby's sense of security and love for the mother; scrubbing the bathroom was not just cleaning but an exercise of maternal instincts, keeping the family safe from disease. As Ann Oakley pointed out some years ago, housewives find it very difficult to disentangle their 'work' from the giving of love and nurturance. To complain about household drudgery is, for most of them, tantamount to saying that they don't love their husbands and children. Complaints about working conditions are reduced to banter as in the 'Merely Men' column in the *Women's Weekly*.

These developments have a long history, but in Australia a key period was the 1920s, the decade of electrification and the rapid spread of appliances. The new technology purported to solve 'the servant problem' by making servants unnecessary. 'Emotionalisation' provided a rationalisation for the middle class woman who was, in most parts of the advanced capitalist world, now stuck with her own housework. (In the upper class and in places like Hong Kong where servants have been retained, housework has *not* been emotionalised.) It also provided a justification for many working class women to leave the workforce and do their *own* domestic work instead of someone else's. The so-called family wage and the expansion of the suburban dream combined with the partial mechanisation of housework to enable even working class men to live 'as if' they had servants. The decline in domestic servants was more than balanced by the increase in fulltime housewives. The *ideal* of the non-working wife was thus consolidated and treated as the norm. The 1920s saw a decline in the proportion of women in the paid workforce. Any slight increase in divorce petitions was counteracted by a rapid rise in the marriage rate and a declining age at marriage (McDonald, 1975: 144–45). By the 1950s the suburban, nuclear family was assumed to be the ideal and inevitable way of organising things. Housework had become not just a job but an expression of love and warmth performed by each woman for her own little family. At the same time new levels of anxiety, guilt and uncertainty began to operate—which are played on all the time by the advertising industry.

The high status given to women's domestic role in the interwar period is reflected in the setting up of Housewives' and Country Women's Associations. At this point housework still retained enough of the old skills to make the new emotional dimensions convincing. After World War II images of domesticity and maternal love were not sufficient settings for consumption and it became more directly sexualised. Women's bodies were increasingly used to sell commodities. Women were not only tied to their role as consumers but more than ever became *objects* of consumption: as sex objects they were expected to find pleasure in pleasing men. These shifts did not threaten the domestic sphere. In fact they went alongside the emotionalisation of housework and the establishment of private life as the place where we 'find our real selves'.

These three advertisements appeared in The Coronation Cookery Book *compiled by the Country Women's Association of New South Wales in 1951. Together they encapsulate a number of the processes that we outline. First, the status of housework in the interwar years: the Rural Bank advertisement is appealing to the idea of the housewife as manager, and the home is being equated with a business establishment. The 'portrait' is like a portrait of a businessman—head with groomed hair and the hint of a collar. The other two advertisements present very different images of women. The Letona ad. points to the beginnings of woman as sex object: 'The pick of the Pantry' is of course herself, rather than the canned peas. The cartoon pin-up form had been prevalent in popular magazines in the interwar period. In the postwar years 'real' women were to replace the cartoon. 'Success' is selling an early version of preprepared foods and points to the beginnings of the deskilling of housework in the postwar period: the success is assured, so that even a schoolgirl can cook with self-raising flour. Preprepared foods have come a long way since the early 1950s, and ways of advertising them have changed considerably, with timesaving taking precedence over success as a cook. Read together these advertisements are contradictory. They represent significant changes taking place in housework in the immediate postwar years: the end of 'housewife as manager' and the beginnings of sexualisation and deskilling that were to characterise the postwar period.*

Portrait of an "Executive"

BOSS of the budget, buyer and business manager for that most important establishment—the HOME.

She knows that to pay bills by Rural Bank cheque is safe, convenient, inexpensive, and business-like.

Your account will be most welcome . . . open it at any branch.

RURAL BANK
OF NEW SOUTH WALES

Head Office: Martin Place, Sydney

"Our business is helping yours!"

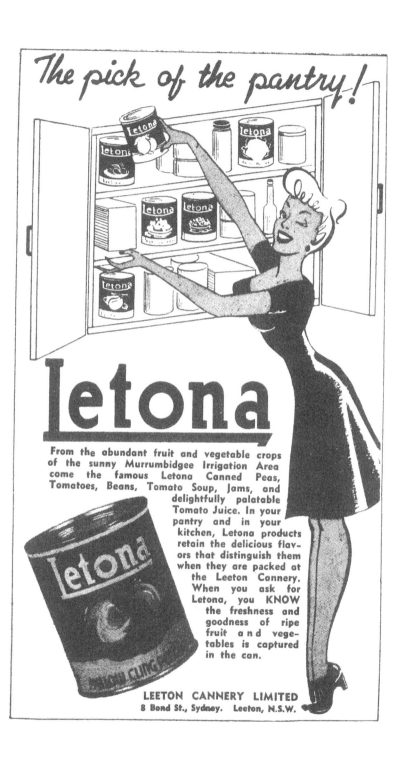

Labour-saving devices did not reduce the time spent on household labour but increased the time available for other family needs and for a larger emotional input (Vanek, 1978: 367–68). Most obviously, families have become a lot more child-centred. Feeding bottles, sterilisers, baby foods, disposable nappies and all the other wonders of modern technology have not reduced the time spent on child care. At times it seems that children too have become objects of consumption, the advantages of another one carefully weighed up against a car, or a holiday, or more money to spend on the existing family. This has been taken a step further as Australian families have actually been able to *buy* babies from Southeast Asia for $3000–$4000—a telling example of the acceptance of the bought over the home-made. While technology may have made the physical care of children easier there has also been a concern with personal development and the discovery of a whole series of *new* children's needs. The two seem to combine in the common practice of chauffeuring children around—a mindless and timewasting task if ever there was one. Such activities counterbalance the reality of smaller families. Concern with the psychological development of children has not improved the status of child care, or at least not that done by the mother. Lasch speaks of the 'proleterianization of parenthood', as housewives were persuaded to rely on outside technology and the advice of experts (1979: 18–19). The 'nurturing mother' had no power base independent of the (male) experts who constituted her as such, invoking new forms of social control and state intervention.

In the postwar period the range of child care options actually declined, placing the burden fair and square on the mother. At the beginning of the century it was spread amongst older children, friends, relatives and neighbours. This changed in the 1920s as the State stepped in to enforce schooling and the old working class communities began to break up. The isolation of mother and children in 'dormitory' suburbs is a relatively recent phenomenon. Although some sociological studies have found evidence of new networks and some interaction in the suburbs this amounts to little more than saying hello to neighbours and lending (but not borrowing) a pound of sugar (Bryson and Thompson, 1972: 109–126; Scott and U'Ren, 1962: 34–35). The very ideal of suburbia was family centredness and leisure activities focussed on the home and garden of the quarter acre block. The reality of working class suburbs is lack of public amenities and facilities, such as transport and parks and playgrounds, and of course, corner shops. This puts considerable limits on the social interaction possible. In the far western suburbs of Sydney, the Housing Commission estates are quite literally dumping grounds for welfare families, a very high proportion of which are single mother families. Their isolation is compounded by economic hardship and a total absence of facilities.

Though consumption is not a private matter, it *is* organised predominantly around individual households. It operates simultaneously within and between households. Not only are class and status marked out in separate consumption rituals; the separate statuses of women and men are marked out, even constituted by their different places in what *appears* to be the same consumption space. While he is watching television she is getting dinner or preparing the next day's sandwiches. Even at the dinner table, she is the one likely to be responsible for serving the food, timing the progression from one course to the next and clearing way. The woman is expected to be a facilitator of other people's consumption rather than (or as well as) an active participant. Consumption workers are required to be almost permanently on-call; and they have to do a large number of repetitive jobs which are spread out in such a way that it is difficult to get blocks of free time. An ex-nurse describes this as very similar to her experience of 'broken shifts'. Another, who works part-time was more explicit: 'in this work we're really looking after big babies. The only difference is that you can walk away when the shift is over—you can't do that with your own baby—I know'.

As both producers and consumers women are predominantly involved in repetitive, high frequency routines, which deny them control over their *time*. If time has become the commodity par excellence, then women's time is undervalued and they have very little of it for themselves. This perhaps sounds contradictory; after all housewives are meant to be their own bosses. They will say that having their own time is one of the advantages of their work. But this free time is largely illusory. As Ann Oakley found in her study of housewives (1976: 92–93). The absence of external supervision means that these women have to supervise their own work; they set themselves tasks and time schedules. Taking leisure is felt to be self-defeating as what is not done today has to be done tomorrow. Housewives' sense of themselves as competent workers is also dependent on organising their time well. Even in this, they are not entirely their own bosses—children and husbands require attention at particular times of the day.

While all of these forces have acted to preserve the sexual division of labour in the domestic sphere, it has not been without contradiction and resistance. As elsewhere, changes in technology in the home mean that the sexual division of labour is constantly under redefinition. To take a clearcut example. The development of feeding bottles and hygienic milk made it perfectly possible for men to feed babies, but this coincided with a redefinition of the 'maternal instinct' accompanied by dire warnings about the effects of 'maternal deprivation' if mother and child were not constantly together. Nonetheless it became harder to assert that the division of labour was based purely on biology.

In some ways the emotional and sexual bonds seem harder to break away from than relations of economic dependence and exploitation.

Here too there are contradictions: notions of companionship and equal partnership in marriage do not rest easily on clearcut role differentiation and inequality; emotional security and sexual excitement are difficult to balance. The emphasis on sex in marriage may have given the institution a new dimension but was not easily containable within it. Eroticism threatens to break out of the existing structures of masculinity and femininity.

As housing prices and interest rates escalate, the suburban ideal is placed beyond the reach of many of the working class or it is possible only on the basis that the wives remain in the paid workforce. This poses a threat to the balance of power within the family, as women earn money which is an important basis of men's power. Inequality becomes more visible as women perform two jobs: the ubiquitous double shift. Their presence in the workforce in large numbers potentially challenges the sexual division of labour outside as well as inside the home. At the same time, their primary position as servants/objects in the consumption sphere has restricted their access to jobs in the paid workforce.

Production/consumption and gender identity

How do women in the workforce negotiate the relation between work and home? This is largely a question of time, or organising work life and domestic life to cope with the demands placed on them in both. But there is more to it. What we are looking at here are two sets of power relations and the interconnections between them. It is commonplace now to say that these power relations are maintained because the sexual division of labour in the workplace and that in the home are mutually reinforcing and are both based on the broad social distinction between wife-mother/breadwinner. In each of our industry studies we have pointed to the complexities in the process of construction of gender identity of women at work. One thing is certain—they do not primarily identify as wives and mothers. Many have a strong sense of their abilities as workers, frequently comparing themselves favourably with men in similar jobs. It is significant that they make this comparison as a way of asserting their capabilities; women's sense of themselves as 'workers' is not *given* in the way that men's is. They have to assert, demonstrate, actively construct their work identity. Men too are active in constructing their work identities but it is from quite a different standpoint in the power relations involved. We have found plenty of evidence of men feeling threatened by women taking their jobs or doing men's work. Their identity as worker/breadwinner is challenged. One of the ways this is resolved is by the redefinition of men's work as women's work or vice versa. If dominance is reasserted it is not a smooth process—women resist in a myriad different ways.

But what of these women at home? How does their participation in the paid workforce affect power relations in the domestic sphere? What is the connection between the construction of their gender identity at work and that at home? We might expect that inequality at home would become more visible if women are performing two jobs. Yet despite the high workforce participation rates of married women there are no apparent changes in the sexual division of labour in the family. Adler found that husbands participated more only when the wife's working role was seen as temporary. When the wife intended to work permanently his contribution was only equivalent to that of the husbands of non-working wives. While the roles will bend somewhat in the face of short-term pressures, permanent alterations are not readily made (Bryson, 1975: 219–20).

One of the most frequent explanations for this is that there is a continuity in the nature of the work that women do in the workplace and the home; that women's work is an extention of their wife-mother role. There are difficulties with this explanation. As we have shown, many women do *not* experience their paid work as an extension of their unpaid. Indeed they frequently make a sharp distinction between these spheres of their lives. And this is not altogether surprising, as one of the defining features of capitalist society is the distinction between work/ non-work, public/private.

The interesting contradiction here is that it is employers who make much of the extension of wife-mother role and attributes to the workplace. The work/non-work split is supposed to apply to men only. The relation between public/private and men/women is more complex than this suggests. When family symbolism is used as a form of control in the workplace, the private sphere is being drawn on directly. It relates to both men and women by reference to the power relation between them in the family.

What we want to suggest here is that women's acceptance of the distinction between public and private has a double-sided effect: on the one hand it is the basis of their constructing a work identity and, on the other, it is the basis of the continuance of a sexual division of labour in the home. This is not as simple as something like a split personality. Rather, it points to the complexities of gender construction. Although women experience a split between the public and the private, their experience is qualitatively different from men's. There are both continuities and discontinuities in the construction of femininity around work and home. Thus the nursing profession, which more than any of the other jobs we considered demands mothering qualities, also has hours which makes it prohibitive for mothers to work in. Nursing administrators are rigid about nurses keeping their work and domestic responsibilities seperate. Nurses are made to feel guilty if they take time off to look after sick children when they are meant to be looking after other sick people. The guilt of mothers is played on, not in connection with their children at home, but their children at work. So much for biology. There is tension between employer's ideological use of continuities between home and work and the very powerful ideology of the work/personal life split under capitalism. The effects are worth considering.

There is little sign of husbands increasing their hours of housework, irrespective of changes in the hours worked either by themselves or their wives. Studies which suggest this is happening have just not looked closely enough and have taken at face value what people *say* is happening. Husbands now like to think they do more in the house, and wives would like to believe it is true. But the reality is different. The husbands of wage-working wives only *appear* to be doing more and it would seem they are kidding themselves. A recent American study showed that on tasks in which they claimed to 'participate' they contributed about ten per cent, on an average, of the time and effort (Hartmann, 1981: 377–83).

An officer in charge in EDP who married late had this to say:

> I am frequently late home—seven or seven-thirty . . . I don't like leaving loose ends at the end of the day. My husband understands—he's also in computing. He insisted I had help in the house, so I don't have to spend my weekends doing housework. I felt uneasy about this at first [having someone come in once a fortnight] but I've got used to it. After all it's creating another industry isn't it? I used to fuss more about housework but now I don't. My husband helped me in that.

She went on to say that they don't eat out much because he likes eating at home. She does all the cooking. This woman is ambitious and was active in pushing women's promotion rights in the late 1960s but it doesn't occur to her that her husband's being 'understanding' could extend to sharing housework, despite the fact that they have similar jobs. It was *her* weekends that were spent doing housework before he persuaded her to get 'help'. Presumably he wants her company in his leisure time. Like nearly all the women in banks who have made it, she does not have children. In this situation, where mothering is not at issue, it might have been expected that inequalities in relation to housework would be more apparent. An administrator in another computer centre, who has always worked and done so 'with [her] husband's support', said that 'he helps me a lot with cooking and shopping. But he draws the line at cleaning the house'. That is, housework proper! Shopping together on Saturday mornings and sometimes cooking are one thing but the drudgery and hard work of cleaning another. Since migrating from England in the 1950s this woman has competently done one job after another—and it would seem has been more successful in her work life than her husband. She also leads a much more active 'leisure' life than he does—bushwalking and painting. Despite this, a power relation is still there. It is not experienced as power; these women accept that they are responsible for housework and think they are fortunate if their husbands help.

There are some differences between women in their fifties, and younger ones in their twenties. The idea that husbands *should* help with housework has become popular and represents something of a shift in anti-feminist ideology. North Shore college students frequently tell us that 'women aren't oppressed any more, men do housework too'. When pressed, it usually turns out that this amounts to putting food in the microwave or Saturday morning shopping. A young trainee programmer claimed that she and her husband shared housework but looked very sheepish about it as if she felt that it should be shared but knew that it really wasn't. She also told us that she has had some hassles with her husband over her work: he doesn't like her taking work home. Women who live with men are usually more cautious about taking work home, or maybe they learn from these experiences. Men taking work home would not be questioned.

It is not at all surprising to find that women who work are expected to take the main responsibilities for domestic work and childcare. Nor would we want to suggest that men sharing housework would end the sexual division of labour in the home. The question of power in the home is not as simple as this, just as in the workplace 'job opportunities' or even 'equal opportunities' for women do not result in a 'balance of power', or an end to the sexual division of labour. Rather than asking why women, particularly those who work outside the home, don't demand more of men, perhaps we should ask why are they reluctant to give up some of their domain to men? The home is supposedly women's world—their space to manage and control.

Not only is it the site of their oppression but also a space defined as theirs to exercise some control over. It is crucial for their identity as the successful shopper, homemaker and childbearer that we have previously discussed. To relinquish these to men would be the last straw. A casual shop assistant expressed this succinctly:

> I don't work just for money. But now we have bought a new house and it costs a lot to furnish—curtains, carpets, soil, grass ... I've developed a buying sense. I handle all the money, make the shopping decisions and pay the bills. He just hands me his money and doesn't have to do anything else.

This woman is 'manager' of the suburban dream and her success at it is very important to her. But she is also not just working to finance it:

> I felt guilty about the baby, but no more. I came to work to get away from baby talk—it's monotonous. Work is good for you and it gives you a chance to talk to men other than your girlfriends' husbands.

Over and over again women told us that they didn't mix work and private life. By this they mean a number of different things: not socialising with people from work, not taking work home, or strictly allocating parts of the week or day for work, and others for personal life.

> I like to keep work and social life separate. Although I am going out with the soft furnishing girls—all of whom have broken marriages.

> You've got to divide the two worlds. I live with my father, brother, sister and her family. We have one baby and we're having another.

> I dislike the term career woman, it implies that that is all there is to you. I keep my work life and private life separate.

> The weekends aren't long enough. I devote the week to work, and do everything else on the weekend—washing, socialising, mowing the lawns.

One exception to this throws light on some of the reasons for making the division. In one EDP centre, the female programmers feel pressure to join the after-work drinking scene:

> There's a lot of socialising at the pub amongst programmers. I feel guilty about it because I'm getting married and buying a house.

There is pressure because programming is still a male domain and women are frequently made to feel uncomfortable in it. Drinking with the men is one way of 'hanging in'. The guilt has two sources: being with men other than her fiance who is a salesperson, and spending money when *she* is responsible for buying a home. This is a nice example of tension arising out of an attempt to maintain a work identity and identity as wife-to-be manager of consumption. It is more usually resolved by keeping the worlds separate, keeping apart the identities as producer and consumer respectively.

This mirrors the general separation in capitalist society between work and personal life but the separation only really fits the *male* experience. The experience of women who work is qualitatively different. Even if they work in feminised occupations, they are occupying what is defined in capitalist society as a male sphere. Home is not simply the refuge it is for men, but another workplace, although not defined as such. Precisely because there is a danger of blurring, women have to establish the distinction even more strongly than men. Where men can allow the two spheres to encroach on each other, taking the division for granted, women cannot. It is analogous to the situation of women doctors or other women in 'men's jobs who have to constantly justify themselves because they do not have patriarchal authority. Men have the power to define what is acceptable and thus feel little tension around the home/work dichotomy. Women are placed on the defensive. They are the ones who have to negotiate the two power structures and the relation between them. And, ironically, they often do this by making an even sharper distinction between them. This makes each area easier to handle. For example, women making it in a man's world are resentful of employers asking them if they're likely to be having children or assuming that they wouldn't move because they're married; they want to be treated as men would be. But of course they *do* have domestic and childcare responsibilities, and the consequence of this kind of strategy for survival at work means that their double shift is not confronted head on. If this strategy makes life at work possible, it also is used to keep peace at home by not bringing work home and not taking up home time with work time in any way. Such means of coping have the effect of reproducing the sexual division of labour. The male experience of the public/private split is not disrupted or contradicted by bringing work home, or workmates or business contacts. On the contrary, these are all means of reasserting his position of power and enforcing acceptance of his other more important outside world from his wife.

For single women the separation functions somewhat differently. For example, they resent the term 'career woman' because it implies that they have given up a lot for the sake of their careers, that they do not have a life outside work. The implication is that they are sexless or can't be real fulfilled women, as if living outside of the nuclear family is an impoverished mode of existence. Keeping personal life separate is a way of asserting and maintaining a sense of self outside work. As one female manager put it 'either you're sexless or you've slept your way to the top'. Maintaining privacy is one way women resist such invasions on their sexuality.

If men's and women's experience of the public/private is not the same, it is also not possible to generalise about women. Their experiences differ according to class position, forms of control in their workplace, and industrial organisation. It is probably not at all surprising that women working in whitegoods talk much more openly about childcare problems and financial difficulties. The basis of their husbands' hostility to their working differs from that of middle class men. One woman who went back to work in a press shop eleven years ago experienced initial hostility from her husband. Her response was 'It's not your fault you don't bring in a family wage. You don't have to be a protector'. Her children, who were nine and ten at the time, were quite happy about her working because they could see that she made new socks and shoes possible; not luxuries but basics.

Women attempting to make it within the male world of a bureaucratic organisation are more likely to make a sharp distinction analagous to the way men do. They frequently forego marriage and children to sustain a rewarding work life but there are middle-class areas of work where the private has become an industrial issue, particularly within the public service and teaching. Maternity leave and childcare have been put on the industrial agenda. In tertiary institutions, students and staff take their children along to classes when holidays don't coincide. In other industries women would face the sack if, in the absence of childcare, they took children to work or stayed at home.

Beyond the production/consumption dichotomy

It seems likely that the sharp distinction between 'work' and 'non-work' (and with it the concept of the [sexual] division of 'labour') only emerged with capitalism (Genovese, 1981; Jolly, 1981). Activities which we would label ritual, leisure or pleasure, *as distinct from* work or production would in other societies blend together as part of the life of the community. If the sexual division of labour in our society is premissed on the split between production and consumption we will need to find ways of ending this split. It will not be sufficient to deal with 'discrimination' at the level of the workplace nor to insist that men share housework. It is clearly not a matter of more equitably distributing a diminishing workload in the consumption sphere. Rather, we must see consumption in qualitative terms and start figuring out ways in which we can resist, intervene in and transform it. This, of course, has implications for the environment and the production process. Instead of living in a world where our 'needs' are determined largely by what the multinationals decide to produce, we might eventually subordinate production to more consciously articulated consumption requirements. Perhaps 'consumer sovereignty' would then mean something.

Women will necessarily be at the forefront of this struggle for it is they who experience the contradictions of the two spheres. As we have said, the system works smoothly for men for it was *made* for them. Women are left permanently off-balance. Patriarchy, in its contemporary form, operates less through the direct authority of the father than through the preservation of these splits: between the 'economy' and the world of nature/culture (the two become fused); between objectivity and subjectivity, the public and the private; and between rationality and emotionality, 'work' and 'leisure'. Women unwittingly preserve the sexual division of labour when they try and keep these areas separate. Meanwhile it is time for men too to examine their own sexuality, emotionality and consumption fantasies. If consumer capitalism is to be transcended we had better start talking about what is to replace it and place examination of the area of consumption high on the agenda.

A new feminist politics

W HEN we began this book our understanding of the sexual division of labour was abstract. We had little idea of the ways in which it shapes people's lives, how it is reproduced day by day through relations at work, and the contradictions involved in this process. What is most striking is the extent of the denial of the sexual division of labour. Everyone 'knows' that computing is not sex-typed and that male and female process workers work side by side. Yet almost in the same breath people will explain why it is 'natural' for men to do some jobs and women to do others. There is an orthodoxy developing that the sexual division of labour is breaking down; that women have 'equal pay' and 'equality of opportunity' and that men help with housework. While the sexual division of labour is changing constantly it is showing a remarkable resilience.

The sexual division of labour is resilient, but not unshakeable or without contradictions. Changes in technology and the labour process always provoke changes in the sexual division of labour, and it is at these points that its basis is most vulnerable, and potentially challengeable. If this division of labour has operated to oppress women, it also gives us many sources of strength from which to overthrow it. Men do not have absolute power in a patriarchal situation—gender relations like class relations are characterised by struggle and resistances. Given the centrality of gender to capitalism, building on the strengths of working class women will be essential in the struggle to create a nonpatriarchal socialist society.

We have said that the sexual division of labour cannot be understood purely in economic terms, and have pointed to the importance of the sexual and the symbolic. This means that it must also be fought at the level of the symbolic. Some may think it indulgent to talk about sexuality when computers are putting people out of work. But what seems impractical may ultimately be practical and what presents itself as practical may not be very practical at all. After all, thousands of jobs have already gone in Australia, and there has not been any notable success in campaigns to save them. To produce more facts and figures on the rate that computers are displacing people may be useful. But it may have the reverse effect of inducing pessimism. One of the whitegoods companies actually showed their workers *Now the Chips are Down* to convince them of the inevitability of new technology. By linking machines and computers to masculine power and sexuality we are delving into the social processes which create the new technology and give it its particular social meaning. This opens up the possibility of finding new ways of achieving changes in the social relations of work.

On the job actions will clearly be central to the struggle against the sexual division of labour and for control over the labour process and technology. Connecting these struggles requires a sensitivity and awareness of the issues. In the last decade, rape, incest and domestic violence have been politicised in this way, and more recently sexual harassment in the workplace has begun to be politicised. Women are starting to speak out about their experiences of harassment and refusing to cop what they have been silent about for years.

The Kelvinator case encapsulates the themes about gender and technology that have been taken up in this book. Kelvinator are attempting to throw women out of the press shops and to get work that they have been doing for decades defined as 'inappropriate for women'. The South Australian Equal Opportunities Commission, and the AMWSU have stood firm; and the Sex Discrimination Board is unlikely to allow an exemption. Kelvinator are reported to be preparing to go to the Federal Arbitration Court for a ruling under the award. This is a blatant case of flouting the state legislation when it suits them to do so. The Kelvinator women need as much support as they can get. In resisting Kelvinator's plans, women (and men) could do much to bring the sexual division of labour to the forefront of political attention and make it possible for others to act in similar situations. This case also points to the importance of defending sections of the State that can be used to confront and contradict the interests of capital and other parts of the State. The NSW government's attack on the Anti-Discrimination Board is testimony to that body's success in this.

Finally, union support in struggles over the sexual division of labour and technology is very important. But it is not helpful to put it in terms of a list of demands on unions. Support will only be achieved if women make the unions their unions. More broadly, we know that as women we will only change things by taking action ourselves: in the workplace and in every aspect of our lives. This is what the experience of the women's liberation movement has taught us. There are countless working class women who know this too, even if they have had no contact with the organised women's movement. Despite, or perhaps because of, the conditions under which they work in shops, factories, banks, offices and hospitals, they demonstrate a strength that opens up possibilities for a new feminist politics.

Bibliography

Australian Bureau of Statistics (1981) *Education, NSW* Canberra
—— (1981) *The Labour Force* Canberra
Australian Institute of Urban Studies (1975) *Housing for Australia: Philosophy and Policies* Canberra: AIUS
Australian Women's Weekly (1960) *The household electrical appliance market in the next ten years* Sydney: Australian Consolidated Press
Barrett, M. (1980) *Women's Oppression Today* London: Verso
Beardon, C. (1980) 'The Political Economy of Computing in Australia' *Journal of Australian Political Economy* No. 7, pp 3–17
Berger, J. (1972) *Ways of Seeing* London: Penguin
Bose, C. (1979) 'Technology and Changes in the Division of Labour in the American Home' *Women's Studies International Quarterly* Nos 2–3, pp 295–304
Braverman, H. (1974) *Labour and Monopoly Capital. The Degradation of Work in the Twentieth Century* New York: Monthly Review Press
Bryson, L. (1975) 'Husband and Wife Interaction in the Australian Family: A Critical Review of the Literature' in J. Mercer (ed.) *The Other Half* Ringwood: Penguin
Bryson, L. and Thompson, F. (1972) *An Australian Newtown: Life and Leadership in a New Housing Suburb* Ringwood: Penguin
Committee of Inquiry into Technological Change in Australia (1980) *Technological Change in Australia* Canberra: AGPS
Carpenter, M. (1977) 'The New Managerialism and Professionalism in Nursing' in M. Stacey, M. Reid, C. Heath and R. Dingwall (eds) *Health in the Division of Labour* London: Croom Helm
Connell, R.W., Ashendon, D.J., Kessler, S. and Dowsett, G.W. (1982) *Making the Difference. Schools, Families and Social Division* Sydney: George Allen & Unwin
Cunningham, L. (1981) 'The Good Mother' in J. Craney and E. Caldwell (eds) *The True Life Story of* —— St Lucia: University of Queensland Press
de Kadt, M. (1979) 'Insurance: A Clerical Work Factory' in A. Zimbalist (ed.) *Case Studies on the Labour Process* New York: Monthly Review Press
Department of Employment and Youth Affairs (1979) *Employment Prospects by Industry and Occupation* Canberra: AGPS
Department of Industry and Commerce (1978) *The Australian Whitegoods Industry* Canberra: AGPS
Department of Labour and Immigration (1975) *Submission to the Industries Assistance Commission Enquiry on Certain Domestic Appliances* Canberra: DLI

Dunstan, K. (1979) *The Store on the Hill* Melbourne: Macmillan

Edwards, R. (1979) *Contested Terrain. The Transformation of the Workplace in the Twentieth Century* New York: Basic Books

Fine, P. (1971) 'Modern Eating Patterns: The Structure of Reality' Paper for AMA Food Science Symposium, New York: November

Galbraith, J.K. (1973) *Economics and the Public Purpose* Boston: Houghton Mifflin

Gamarnikow, E. (1978) 'Sexual Division of Labour: The Case of Nursing' in A. Kuhn and A. Wolpe *Feminism and Materialism* London: Routledge and Kegan Paul

Game, A. and Pringle, R. (1979) 'Sexuality and the Suburban Dream' *ANZJS* Vol. 15 No. 2 July pp 4–15

Game, A. and Pringle, R. (1980) 'Women, the Labour Process and Technological Change in the Banking Industry' in G.J. Crough (ed.) *Money, Work and Social Responsibility. The Australian Financial System* Sydney: TCRP, University of Sydney

Genovese E.F. (1981) 'Women and Work' Unpublished paper Binghamton: Fernand Braudel Center, SUNY

Gilding, M. (1982) 'Economic Relations in the Bourgeois Family, Sydney, 1870–1940' *Bicentennial History Bulletin, Family History* No. 9 April pp 66–71

Giddens, A. (1973) *The Class Structures of Advanced Societies* London: Hutchinson

Greenbaum, J. (1979) *In the Name of Efficiency. Management Theory and Shopfloor Practice in Data Processing Work* Philadelphia: Temple University Press

Harper, J. and Richards, L. (1979) *Mothers and Working Mothers* Ringwood: Penguin

Hartmann, H. (1981) 'The Family as the Focus of Gender, Class and Political Struggle: The Example of Housework' *Signs* Vol. 6 No. 3 pp 377–83

Hobbs, V. (1979) *But Westward Look. Nursing in Western Australia 1829–1979* Perth: University of Western Australia Press for the Royal Australian Nursing Federation (WA Branch)

Industries Assistance Commission (1978) *Domestic Refrigerating Appliances etc* Canberra: AGPS

Jacka, M. and Game, A. (1980) 'The Whitegoods Industry: The Labour Process and the Sexual Division of Labour' Sydney: Macquarie University

Jacka, M. and Pringle, R. (1981) 'Survey of Workers in the Whitegoods Industry' Sydney: Macquarie University

Jolly, M. (1981) 'The Sexual Division of Labour—Of Public and Private Parts' Unpublished paper Sydney: School of Behavioural Sciences, Macquarie University

Johnston, R.J. and Rimmer, P.J. (1969) *Retailing in Melbourne* Canberra: Research School of Pacific Studies, ANU

Kemeny, J. (1977) 'The Ideology of Home Ownership' *Arena* No. 46 pp 81–89

Kraft, P. (1977) *Programmers and Managers. The Routinisation of Computer Programming in the United States* New York: Springer-Verlag

Lansbury, R. (1980) 'New Technology and Industrial Relations in the Retail Grocery Trade' *Journal of Industrial Relations* Vol. 22 No. 3 pp 275–292

Lasch, C. (1979) *Haven in a Heartless World. The Family Besieged* New York: Basic Books

Law, G. (1980) ' "I have never liked Trade Unionism": The Development of the Royal Australian Nursing Federation, Queensland Branch, 1904–45' in E. Windschuttle *Women, Class and History* Melbourne: Fontana

Macculloch, J. (1980) ' "This store is our world". Female Shop Assistants in Sydney to 1930' in J. Roe (ed.) *Twentieth Century Sydney Studies in Urban and Social History* Sydney: Hale and Iremonger

McDonald, P.F. (1975) *Marriage in Australia* Canberra: ANU Press

Middleton, M.R. (1957) 'Trends in Family Organisation in Australia' in O.A. Oeser and S.B. Hammond *Social Structure and Personality in a City* London: Routledge and Kegan Paul

Nakano Glenn, E. and Feldberg, R. (1979) 'Proletarianising Clerical Work: Technology and Organisational Control in the Office' in A. Zimbalist (ed.) *Case Studies on the Labour Process* New York: Monthly Review Press

Nursing Personnel Survey, Report of the Committee on (1979) *Nursing Personnel A National Survey* Volumes 1 and 2 Canberra: Commonwealth Department of Health, AGPS

Oakley, A. (1976) *Housewife* Harmondsworth: Penguin

Pratt, A. (1978) *Sidney Myer* Melbourne: Quartet

Pringle, R. (1981) 'The Sexual Division of Labour in Computing' *Journal of Australian Political Economy* No. 10 June pp 23–35

Sargeant, L. (ed.) (1981) *Women and Revolution: A Discussion of the Unhappy Marriage of Marxism and Feminism* Boston: South End Press

Sennett, R. (1980) *Authority* New York: Alfred A. Knopf

Scott, D. and U'Ren, R. (1962) *Leisure. A Social Enquiry into Leisure Activities and Needs in an Australian Housing Estate* Melbourne: Cheshire

The Task Force Established by the Minister for Education (1981) *The Role and Function of the Enrolled Nursing Aide in New South Wales* Sydney

Tertiary Education Commission (1978) *Nurse Education and Training* Canberra: The Committee of Inquiry into Nurse Education and Training

Townend, C. (1981) 'Sunning by the Pool' in J. Craney and E. Caldwell (eds) *The True Life Story of* ——St Lucia: University of Queensland Press

Vanek, J. (1977) 'Time Spent in Housework' *Scientific American* November pp 116–20

Vanek, J. (1978) 'Household Technology and Social Status: Rising Living Standards and Status and Residence Differences in Housework' *Technology and Culture* Vol. 19 No. 3 July pp 361–75

West, J. (1978) 'Women, Sex and Class' in A. Kuhn and A. Wolpe (eds) *Feminism and Materialism* London: Routledge and Kegan Paul

Whiteside, T. (1978) 'Din-Din' in J.D. Gussow (ed.) *The Feeding Web: Issue in Nutritional Ecology* Palo Alto: Bull Publishing Co

Women's Employment Rights Campaign (1979) *Women and Unemployment* Sydney: WERC

Index

www.ingramcontent.com/pod-product-compliance
Ingram Content Group UK Ltd.
Pitfield, Milton Keynes, MK11 3LW, UK
UKHW020416010325
455677UK00029B/906

9 780868 612614